POLITICS IN WISCONSIN

Politics
in Wisconsin

Leon D. Epstein

The University of Wisconsin Press

Madison, 1958

Published by The University of Wisconsin Press,
430 Sterling Court, Madison 6, Wisconsin

Copyright © 1958,
by the Regents of the University of Wisconsin

Copyright, Canada, 1958
Distributed in Canada by Burns and MacEachern, Toronto

Printed in the United States of America
by Vail-Ballou Press, Inc., Binghamton, N.Y.

Library of Congress Catalog Card No. 58–13445

For Two Long-time Wisconsin Voters

MY MOTHER AND FATHER

Preface

COLLECTING and tabulating the data for this work took place over several years, and I had the help of many hands. At one time or another, research assistance was provided by the following graduate students in political science at the University of Wisconsin: Bonnie Reese, Howard Martin, Donald Kommers, Harold Haak, and Jan Marfyak. I am grateful to them all for tedious tasks intelligently performed, and especially to Harold Haak, who was burdened with the largest number of those chores. Two other graduate students, Samuel Patterson and Assemblyman Wilder Crane, afforded specialized counsel, and Assemblyman Crane many insights from his own legislative experience. In addition, my wife often served as a research aide as well as a most helpful critic and proofreader of the manuscript.

I have depended on the professional advice of numerous colleagues at the University of Wisconsin, and especially on the generous help of Professors Burton Fisher, Ralph Huitt, Edwin Witte, Clara Penniman, Malcolm MacLean, and Douglas Marshall. As readers of the manuscript, both Professors V. O. Key, Jr., of Harvard University and Heinz Eulau of Antioch College made valuable suggestions based on their own expertness in the kind of study attempted here. Furthermore I am indebted to several newspapermen and many Wisconsin politicians—legislators, candidates, and party officials—who were good enough to give me their time either for interviews or mail questionnaires.

Financial assistance came from the Graduate Research Committee and the College of Letters and Science of the University of Wisconsin during the summer of 1955 and from the Committee on Political Behavior of the Social Science Research Council during seven months of 1957. The latter assistance was for research on the recruitment of political personnel in Wisconsin, and the Social Science Research Council made it possible for the research to be undertaken collaboratively with similar projects in other states. In particular, I am grateful for the research conferences which were arranged in 1956 and 1957 because they enabled me to benefit from the suggestions of my collaborators studying the politics of other states: Clement Vose, Henry Bain, Lester Seligman, Charles Judah, and Joseph Schlesinger. Also, during the course of my research in 1957, I was fortunate to attend an intellectually stimulating Conference on Comparative State Politics, arranged by Professor James K. Pollock at the University of Michigan.

While all of the conferences, committees, and individuals named above were valuable contributors to this enterprise, I must assume sole responsibility for the contents of the book.

For permission to reproduce in revised form material previously published, I want to make the following acknowledgments: for much of Chapter Three, to the editor of the *Journal of Politics* (Vol. 18, August, 1956); for much of Chapter Four, to the editor of the *Western Political Quarterly* (Vol. IX, March, 1956); for parts of Chapter Five, to the editor of the *Midwest Journal of Political Science* (Vol. I, Nov., 1957) and to the editor and the publisher (Clarendon Press, Oxford) of *Political Studies* (Vol. IV, Feb., 1956).

LEON D. EPSTEIN

Madison, Wisconsin
February, 1958

Contents

ix

x *Contents*

Tables

Figures

POLITICS IN WISCONSIN

CHAPTER I

Introduction

THIS is a study of politics in a single state, but it is not the uniqueness of Wisconsin's politics which is to receive primary attention. This applies to personalities and to institutions. Although there are special features of Wisconsin politics that must be noted, these features are not meant to obscure the fact that political behavior in the state is of a species with that in the other forty-seven states, and of a genus with that in other democratic nations. It is political behavior generally that remains of first concern even though the subject matter is confined to Wisconsin. Thus most of the research represented in this volume has been directed to broad propositions which might be tested, and in some instances have been tested, in other states as well. The object, in other words, is comparative despite the limitation that results from confinement of the study to Wisconsin data. I may add that this approach derives from my own continued research interest in using the comparative method of analysis in studying European, particularly British, politics in relation to American.

It is hoped that the findings of the work will contribute to the systematic accumulation of knowledge in the field of state politics. Consistently with such a purpose, an attempt has been made to direct much of the Wisconsin research along lines already projected by other scholars in the field and particularly to follow certain inquiries suggested by V. O. Key.[1] Many of Key's hypotheses, based on his study of several states, are used here as a frame of reference in examining Wisconsin data.

That American state politics, whether studied illustratively in a single state or in several states, is a significant subject of inquiry seems almost beyond dispute. The case rests not only on the growing number and complexity of state governmental functions, but also on the close relation of state parties and elections to national politics. Without in any way understating the powerful impact of national influences on state affairs—an impact to be examined in this work—it is nevertheless also true that state political systems decisively affect national concerns. As is well known, our national parties remain essentially federations of state organizations. And national politicians must ordinarily serve their apprenticeships at the state level.

By concentrating on some general aspects of state politics as illustrated by Wisconsin experience, instead of studying special features of the state's political history, many interesting and important subjects have had to be put to one side. In particular, only passing attention is accorded the fascinating question, asked most often by observers of Wisconsin, of how a state that elected the progressive La Follettes could subsequently have elected McCarthy. Even though this work is mainly concerned with the postwar decade, Senator McCarthy's own career receives no extended separate treatment. The reasons for this relative neglect of Wisconsin's most conspicuous postwar figure are various. First, to do the individual subject justice would require a full-scale biographical account, which, while it might be most illuminating with respect to American political careers, is still impossible without special access to personal records. Second, "McCarthyism" as a political phenomenon belonged to the nation and not only to Wisconsin. In fact, its impact on the political and cultural life of the state was not particularly great. McCarthy, unlike the elder La Follette, never headed an organization which controlled or heavily influenced the state government. Furthermore, McCarthy's electoral support at his re-election in 1952, the one occasion when the issue of McCarthyism was directly presented to Wisconsin voters, proved to be much less than that of other Republican candidates. Third, an analysis of McCarthy's vote on that occasion, while interesting for the light it throws on the varying strength of his appeal to different areas, has already been published and is, in any case, somewhat tangential to the main lines of inquiry established here.[2]

Another limitation on the scope of the present work flows from the method employed. Political narrative, despite its potential interest, has been almost eliminated except as necessary background material, and the anecdotal possibilities have been put aside. Instead attention is concentrated on testing specific hypotheses, often relating to fairly narrow subject matter. While this may seem annoyingly or pretentiously scientific, it is consistent with the objective of presenting political findings in a way that is orderly and subject to check by other investigators in other research situations. Given this objective, it has been convenient to rely heavily on such political data as are capable of quantitative measurement. By no means does this indicate a belief that quantitative studies can exhaust the knowable in politics. It is only that studies of this sort are especially suitable for the present limited purpose.

In developing the several sets of hypotheses made explicit in subsequent chapters, it is fair to say that a political model has been kept consciously in mind. This model is of a democratic political system ordinarily supposed to function with two well-organized and well-defined parties competing fairly evenly for state as well as national offices. That such a competitive order is the most desirable form of political democracy, or even the only form consistent with democracy, is widely taken for granted at least in the United States and Great Britain. Competition for office in and of itself is assumed virtually without question to be an essential in making popular choice meaningful, and competition between parties is the distinctively modern form which it is only somewhat less universally thought that competition must take. That there should be but two major parties is a familiar Anglo-American conception, and that these parties should be sufficiently cohesive so as to accept "responsibility" for presenting and carrying out programs is part of the model as understood by many political scientists. On this latter score, the actual model is usually provided by British parties and is urged on American parties as a norm not so far achieved. Although the author has decided reservations about the feasibility of some aspects of this two-party competitive model, it does serve as a point of departure for much of the present study. The hypotheses employed ordinarily express degrees of conformity to or deviation from expectations associated with organized two-party competition.

Some preview of the range of topics is in order. Following the present essentially methodological introductory chapter, there is in Chapter Two another kind of necessary preliminary —a broad sketch of the Wisconsin setting. The purpose is to describe the social and economic environment in which the state's political system operates. This implies an admission of the obvious: that Wisconsin, like any other state, must be less than an ideal scientific laboratory. The setting of one state is not exactly replicated elsewhere, and therefore what is learned about Wisconsin politics cannot be assumed, in advance of comparable studies, to hold in states whose politics may be conditioned by different general settings. This is not to contradict the bold statement of this chapter's first paragraph that Wisconsin political behavior is of a species with that of the other forty-seven states, but it is to suggest the possibility that politics in Wisconsin, in addition to having something in common with politics elsewhere, may also have characteristics which would be found only in states whose general settings closely resemble Wisconsin's.

The plain and unhappy fact confronting the political scientist is that he can never abstract his subject matter from social and economic circumstances. Politics always operates in a given environment that is not of the student's making, and he has to allow for a variety of independent variables which may decisively influence behavior differently on different occasions. While unquestionably this complicates the task of scientific inquiry, it need not cause its abandonment. The simplest way to deal with environmental factors is to indicate what they are, and thus make it possible for them to be taken into account in comparative studies. Any way in which the Wisconsin setting resembles or differs from that of other states may help to explain similarities and differences in political behavior.

The remainder of the work is concerned with political analysis of certain selected topics. First, the state's party system is broadly examined in terms of its past deviations from and its more recent tendencies toward the two-party model. It is in this chapter that the political history of the state is briefly reviewed, but the principal concern is to explain the party system of the postwar decade. The background is designed to put the politics of 1946–1956 in an intelligible perspective, and especially to emphasize the novelty of the postwar pattern of two-party competition.

Subsequent chapters are more specialized. There is a detailed analysis of the postwar two-party vote on the basis of the breakdown according to size of place. Party organizations are then described with particular attention accorded local units and their officers. State legislators and their selection provide the material for Chapters Six and Seven. In each of these several specialized chapters, research has been concentrated on relatively few aspects of each subject so that a complete description, for example, of the Wisconsin legislature, the election process, or the party machinery is not attempted. The book is not meant to be a general introduction to Wisconsin government and politics. It remains to be added that in the concluding chapter there is a review of some of the broader implications of the particular research findings.

A few themes will be found to recur in several chapters. One of these concerns the direct primary method of nomination, especially appropriate, it might be noted, for analysis here in light of Wisconsin's long experience with the institution. The significance of this analysis may be most fully understood by recalling how characteristically American it is for party candidates to be chosen in primary elections instead of in party gatherings of some sort. That candidates are so generally nominated by this method in the United States but not elsewhere is one of the most striking distinguishing features of the American political system. As such, it is examined here in its historical association with a one-party system, and as a substitute for two-party competition at various levels of election.

Related to this theme is the even more general one of the function of party organization with respect to the selection of candidates. Control by the party of its own nominations is an essential element of the previously described political model, particularly in its emphasis on the desirability of party responsibility for policies and programs. Yet it is agreed that this is not regularly achieved in the United States. Wisconsin is by no means presented as an exception. Rather data drawn from the state's political experience illustrate the extent to which the model is departed from, and how such a departure may be so substantial as to provide some basis for an alternative model of political behavior to that customarily advanced.

A third recurrent theme is the distinction between urban and rural political styles. Certain refinements are introduced in the use of the two terms, *urban* and *rural,* and for some purposes a breakdown within each category is employed. This is particularly evident in the chapter analyzing the division of the two-party vote by size of place and in the later material on the character of legislative districts. A more general urban-rural distinction is made in the discussion of party organizations and individual legislators. The assumption underlying all such distinctions is that urban and rural environments, though within a single state, make for significantly different political practices, and the object here is to learn the extent to which this is the case.

It is well at this point to emphasize the limited period of time with which this work is concerned. Primarily it is the postwar decade, 1946–1956. Within this period the legislative election of 1956, along with party organizations as of that election year, receives special attention. Since most of the research was conducted between 1955 and 1957, and the writing mainly done in mid-1957, there are but few references to the upset special senatorial election victory by the Democratic candidate in 1957 and no references at all to events in 1958. Concern, then, is largely with an era in which two-party competition still took the form of regular Republican majorities, and much of the work is necessarily devoted to an explanation of the maintenance of those majorities. As of late 1957, it is possible to believe that this explanation may no longer appropriately be put in the present tense. It is at least conceivable that Democratic majorities will be established in 1958 or 1960, and thus the present description of the postwar pattern will appear largely as an historical account. This is an inevitable risk for the political scientist who uses recent data, and he guards best against the embarrassment of political overturns by admitting that they are indeed possible. At any rate, the intention is really to present findings which, while derived from a particular era, are nonetheless relevant, though modest, contributions to an understanding of politics generally. For example, the description of Republican dominance in postwar Wisconsin experience is meant to throw some light on the broad nature and consequences of traditional one-party majorities. Although some of the topical significance of this discussion would be lost if Republican dominance were ended in Wisconsin, there should remain whatever value the study has by way of general insight into the political process in situations like that of postwar Wisconsin—that is, where a traditional majority party met the challenge of a new opposition.

This is the appropriate place for a note about methods of research. Only a relatively small amount of information has been gathered by the traditional scholarly use of written sources —newspapers, documents, and the like. This is apart from the heavy reliance on official election records and census publications. Field investigation has constituted the major research effort, and it has included standardized interviews, mail questionnaires, observation of political meetings, and a considerable number of informal talks with political participants. One particular part of this field investigation is worth special note here because its contribution to the work may not otherwise be apparent. Five counties, chosen for their representativeness in terms of urban-rural status, political background, and degree of party competition, were studied intensively with respect to the selection of legislative candidates in 1956. In this variety of situations, the relation of local party organizations to primary and general election campaigns was examined, and illustrative material provided for generalizations that appear to have been established by the broader but less microscopic state-wide findings. The detailed field inquiry also served to develop hypotheses for state-wide examination and to give some feeling for local political situations. In each of the five selected counties, legislative candidates and other politicians were interviewed, and the course of the 1956 campaign was studied from a variety of oral and written sources. The resulting data have been put in the form of reports on each county, but these reports are too particularized for inclusion in this volume.

Finally an explanation is needed for the manner in which the tabulated material of this volume is presented. In order to make the presentation complete and yet avoid the high cost of printing all forty-six tables in the text, most of the tabulation is contained in an especially prepared Appendix. Tables in this Appendix are referred to in the text by chapter number and letter (i.e., II-A, VI-P) so that the data-conscious reader can readily consult the material at the back of the book. However, an effort has been made to provide more than the usual amount of textual exposition of the data contained in Appendix tables, and thus to limit the paging back and forth. Where this was particularly difficult to accomplish, namely in the case of six key tables, such tables are printed in the chapters to which they relate and are designated by ordinary arabic numerals.

CHAPTER II

The Wisconsin setting

Two sets of Wisconsin characteristics are described in this chapter. The first deals with social and economic aspects of the state, and the second with certain relatively fixed political institutions. It is appreciated that these two sets of characteristics differ from each other in kind, and that the institutional features are less basic. There may even seem something odd about treating political institutions along with social and economic characteristics as though they were all independent variables in a study of politics. Political institutions themselves are usually taken to be dependent variables, as they are in subsequent portions of this book. However, certain institutional features of Wisconsin politics are so firmly established by constitution or custom that they provide part of the environmental setting for political behavior in a way that is at least analogous to the influence of social and economic characteristics. To omit a description of such institutions would be to disregard an essential part of the frame of reference in which this study is set.

SOCIAL AND ECONOMIC CHARACTERISTICS

Population: size and growth

Wisconsin is a medium-sized American state in population. Ranking fourteenth, Wisconsin's total, in 1950, of just under three and one-half million people places the state well below the seven largest states (New York, California, Pennsylvania, Illinois, Ohio, Texas, and Michigan) but in roughly the same

11

class with the six other states larger than Wisconsin, none of which is over five million. Also, it may be observed, Wisconsin's population is in the range of the smaller European countries, specifically Ireland, Norway, Switzerland, and Denmark. By American standards, Wisconsin's recent population growth has been steady but not remarkably large. Its increase from 1940 to 1950 was 9.5 per cent, which was below the national average of 14.5 per cent and which placed Wisconsin thirtieth among the states (and the District of Columbia) in percentage increase during the decade.[1] The state's rate of increase had been greater in the decades before 1930, and particularly before 1920 when there was still a large in-migration to Wisconsin. Between 1940 and 1950, however, 86,000 more people moved out of the state than moved in, and it was only the excess of births over deaths that caused a net increase in Wisconsin population. The same general trends have been estimated as holding good in the 1950's.[2] It is plain, then, that Wisconsin is not a boom state. Neither is it depressed. The out-migration is not so large as to prevent a steady increase, resulting from the excess of births over deaths, in the total population.

However, this generalization concerning gradual growth holds only for the state taken as a unit. Almost all of the increase of recent years has been concentrated in the southern and eastern sections of the state, long the most highly populated. Much of the rest of the state actually lost population between 1940 and 1950. This decrease is especially marked in the poorer rural counties of northern and northwestern Wisconsin. The southern and eastern counties not only have most of the urban industrial development but also the agricultural advantages of better soil, a longer growing season, and proximity to metropolitan markets. In the section that can be marked off in a southeastern triangle of the state (Figure 1) by drawing a line along the western edges of Brown, Outagamie, Winnebago, Fond du Lac, Dodge, Dane, and Green counties, there are 19 counties (of the state's 71) with 60.4 per cent of the state's population (as of 1950) in only 18.6 per cent of the state's land area.[3] Outside of this area there is no city as large as 50,000, although there are some smaller growing urban centers as well as several fertile and thriving agricultural counties. It is mainly in the northern third of the state that there is general stagnation or decline of population.

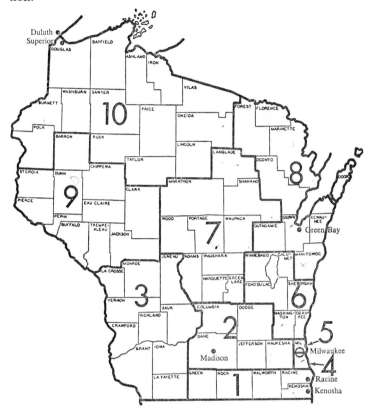

Figure 1.—Wisconsin Counties, Congressional Districts, and Cities over 50,000 (counting Superior with Duluth urbanized area)

Urban-and-rural pattern

Urbanization has been a marked feature of Wisconsin's population as it has of growing areas elsewhere. Nevertheless the state remains less urban than the United States as a whole. In 1950 the state's population, according to the U.S. Census definition, was 57.9 per cent urban, compared to 64.0 per cent in the entire country. Wisconsin's still substantial rural percentage, however, is hardly synonymous with farm population.

Only about one-fifth of the state's total population actually live on farms, and this proportion is smaller than the number, also rural by Census definition, who live in nonfarm places under 2,500. Furthermore the farm population has declined absolutely as well as relatively in every decade since 1920 and is continuing to do so in the 1950's. This tendency, along with the growth in the urban and the rural nonfarm populations, is typical of much of the United States.

Wisconsin's urbanization does have one distinctive feature. Appreciably less of the state's population is concentrated in a few large centers than is true of much of the rest of urban America. Or, stated affirmatively, more of Wisconsin's urban population is in small and medium-sized cities (under 50,000) than is usually the case in large industrial states. This may conveniently be shown for 1950 by adding "urbanized areas," the Census term for certain cities over 50,000 plus their urban fringes, and any other cities over 50,000, thus getting a population that may be called a "metropolitan" component of the Census-defined total urban population. Calculations, expressed in percentages, appear below in Table 1 for the United States and for selected states along with Wisconsin.[4]

Table 1

COMPARATIVE URBANIZATION

Per cent of total population in:	U.S.	Ill.	Iowa	Kan.	Mich.	Minn.	Neb.	N.Y.	Wis.
Urbanized areas and other cities over 50,000	46.8	62.5	22.0	24.3	57.9	36.6	27.8	76.7	33.7
All urban places	64.0	77.6	47.7	52.1	70.7	54.5	46.9	85.5	57.9

It may be observed that Wisconsin's population percentage in the plus-50,000 category is farther below that for the country and for the larger states than is the case in comparing percentages for all urban places. And relative to Minnesota the Wisconsin percentage in the larger cities is lower although its percentage in all urban places is higher. These statistics, it is easy to explain, are a function of the fact that Wisconsin's one very large urbanized area, Milwaukee, has less than one-fourth the state's population and thus bulks smaller in Wisconsin than do major population centers in Michigan, Minnesota, Illinois, or New York. In other terms, Wisconsin is urban, even if less than the nation, but not highly metropolitan. Cities between 2,500 and 50,000, all technically urban, constitute a relatively large portion of Wisconsin's total population, in fact about one-fourth.

This somewhat deconcentrated urbanism may cushion the impact of the reduction of rural Wisconsin to a minority status. Technically the rural population has constituted less than half the total since the 1930 Census, but the social significance of the change, particularly in the reduction of the farm population percentage, has become more apparent in the 1950's. It was illustrated in dramatic form by the adoption of daylight-saving time in a popular referendum in 1957. Only ten years before, rural Wisconsin's traditional dislike of setting the clocks ahead had been substantially confirmed by referendum, and therefore the 1957 poll of 54.6 per cent in favor of daylight-saving time represented a new and impressive display of urban voting power. As may be seen from Table II-A and Figure 2, only 21 of Wisconsin's 71 counties voted for the change, but their votes were sufficient to overcome all the rest of the state despite very high percentages against daylight saving in the heavily rural counties. Especially noteworthy is the fact that Milwaukee County alone more than made up for the majority polled by the opposition in the rest of the state. However, there would not likely be many issues on which the metropolitan population would be so nearly united regardless of party. The cow was no longer king, but neither was a thoroughly urban hegemony established.

Instead the character and rate of Wisconsin's urbanization make it likely that for several decades the rural cultural pattern will remain a seriously contending force in the affairs of the state. That pattern, it should be noted, differs from the urban in certain significant ways. The population of rural Wisconsin is older and has received fewer years of schooling than that of the cities. The age differential arises from the fact that younger people move in great numbers from both farms and villages to cities, while older people, if they move from farms at all, tend to move to villages rather than to urban areas. The educational difference is reflected in the higher figure of median years of school completed by those in urban areas, and it is also illustrated by the fact that in 1950 the percentage of Wisconsin's urban sixteen- and seventeen-year-olds actually in school ranked first in the United States while the comparable percentage of rural youth ranked twenty-third in the country.[5] These differentials in age and in education suggest the kind of contrast between a dynamic society and a static society that can be significantly reflected in political conflict.

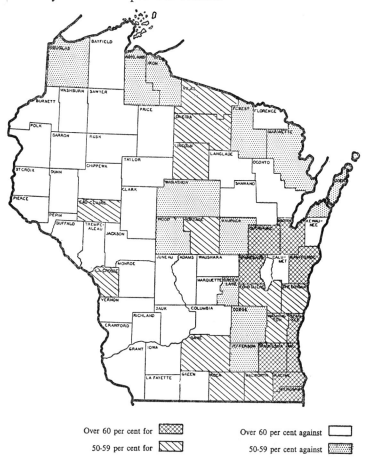

Over 60 per cent for   Over 60 per cent against

50-59 per cent for   50-59 per cent against

Figure 2.—Urban-Rural Political Index: Daylight-Saving Time Referendum (April, 1957)

Ethnic background

The earliest large movement of population into Wisconsin was of Yankee origin, and the cultural and political influence of New England and upstate New York was decisive during the middle decades of the nineteenth century when the state's institutions (like the New England town along with the county unit) were adopted. Even then, however, there were many immigrants from continental Europe, and the number became much larger between 1870 and 1910, as it did in many other parts of the United States.[6] The period and the scale of European immigration to Wisconsin are not unique, but the state's total immigration stands relatively high when, as of 1930, a count is made of those who were foreign-born or of foreign-born or mixed parentage. In this category were 50.3 per cent of the state's total population.[7] This put Wisconsin above Illinois (45.8 per cent) but below New York (61.0 per cent). It meant that in this respect at least Wisconsin has more in common with these large industrial states than with Iowa, Kansas, and Nebraska, for instance, which had much lower percentages foreign-born or of foreign-born or mixed parentage.[8] It should be noted that Wisconsin's nineteenth-century immigrants from Europe settled in large numbers on farms as well as in manufacturing cities. Thus in 1930 the percentage foreign-born or of foreign-born or mixed parentage in Milwaukee County (59.6 per cent) was not so much higher than the percentage (47.2) in the rest of the state.

The most striking characteristic of Wisconsin's ethnic pattern is also the best-known: the predominance of Germans. Again taking the 1930 national origins calculation of foreign-born and native of foreign-born or mixed parentage, 41.2 per cent of this total were of German origin. Or, stated differently, German ethnic background thus measured accounted for 20.7 per cent of the state's total population in 1930. German immigration to Wisconsin began before 1850 and continued on a large scale through the rest of the nineteenth century. Although falling behind southern and eastern European immigration in the first decades of the twentieth century, the German figure was again in first place during the lighter immigration years from 1920 to

1930.[9] German immigrants were numerous enough over time so as to be located in many parts of the state, but the largest concentrations have been in Milwaukee and in the agriculturally rich eastern counties, particularly from Jefferson and Waukesha north to Outagamie and Brown counties. It is in these counties that one still finds villages and rural towns that are almost solidly German in ethnic background.

The next most numerous ethnic group, according to the 1930 calculation, is Polish, but the percentage of foreign-born or native of foreign-born or mixed parentage who were Polish was only 9.4 per cent compared to the 41.2 per cent previously cited for Germans. Nevertheless Wisconsin's population of Polish descent has considerable significance because of its later arrival and its heavy concentration in the industrial areas of Milwaukee and in a few rural counties. In 1930 over half of those' of Census-defined Polish origin lived in Milwaukee County, and constituted about ten per cent of that county's total population.

Almost as large as the Polish population is the Norwegian, which in 1930 comprised 9.2 per cent of the foreign-born or native of foreign-born or mixed parentage. If the percentages of Swedes (3.9) and Danes (2.8) are added to the Norwegian figure, the total Scandinavian population is obviously impressive. It is to be found in various sections of the state, but, especially in the case of the Norwegians, most heavily in Dane County and in the counties to the northwest of Dane. The largest Scandinavian immigration was from 1850 to 1880, and thus it coincided with a period of heavy German immigration.

Generally the predominance, established in the nineteenth century, of people of northern European descent—Yankees, Germans, and Scandinavians—was not greatly changed by the population movements at the turn of the century. It is true that in addition to the large Polish migration Wisconsin did attract other southern and eastern Europeans, Czechoslovakians and Italians in particular, but their total numbers were not sufficient to establish large state-wide ethnic groupings. Locally, of course, one of these ethnic groups may have a special importance. The same, only more decisively, may be said for Negroes in Wisconsin. Their numbers have traditionally been very small, and, despite recent increases, the Negro population was less than one per cent of the state's total in 1950. It is plain that Wisconsin remains overwhelmingly populated by the descendants of northern Europeans. The point should be emphasized so that the relatively high percentage of foreign-born or native of foreign-born or mixed parentage does not lead one to visualize Wisconsin as a state heavily populated by the great southern and eastern European immigration of the turn of the century.

Religion

As well as it can be estimated on the basis of the last published religious census (1936), Wisconsin has a relatively high percentage of Catholics. In terms of the state's estimated population in 1936, Catholics constituted 24.5 per cent of the total.[10] This is a higher proportion than has been calculated on a similar basis for Illinois (18.6 per cent) and New York (23.4 per cent).[11] The explanation for Wisconsin's high figure lies partly in the fact that there are many German Catholics, as well as many German Lutherans, in the state. The Catholic population is both urban and rural. In particular, it should be noted that, unlike some industrial states, Wisconsin's metropolitan center contains hardly any more Catholics than does the rest of the state. In 1936 the percentage of Catholics in Milwaukee County was 26.9 compared to 23.6 outstate.[12]

Among the Protestant majority, the largest religious group consists of the several Lutheran denominations. This is pretty much as expected of a population so heavily German and Scandinavian in ethnic background. The Jewish minority, it might be added, is small, amounting to only 1.2 per cent of the 1936 population, and highly concentrated in Milwaukee County (where it constituted 3.8 per cent of the population).

Economy

Wisconsin is not one of the wealthiest states, but neither is it poor by comparison to most of the country. Its median income, as of 1950, was above the national average and ranked fourteenth among the states.[13] Without any large economically depressed population, except possibly for the diminishing number of marginal farmers in the northern counties, the state combines agricultural and urban industrial prosperity in a way that is similar in general to that of the other states of the Census's East North Central, or Great Lakes, region (Ohio, Indiana, Illinois, and Michigan). However, while Wisconsin is fairly counted part of this region in census classification, it is marginally so in an economic as well as a strictly geographic sense. Located as it is on the wrong side of Lake Michigan as far as eastern population centers are concerned, Wisconsin has much in common with Minnesota as well as with the more highly industrialized East North Central states. Agriculture is proportionately more important in Wisconsin than it is in Ohio, Indiana, Illinois, or Michigan. The state's economy is that of a borderland between the more industrial East and the more agricultural prairie West. Significantly, within the state, manufacturing is heavily concentrated on the eastern lakeshore.

Perhaps because a higher proportion of Wisconsin employment than of national employment is in agriculture, it is still usual to begin any discussion of elements in the Wisconsin economy with agriculture even though it now employs little more than one-fifth of the state's employable males. Farming thus ranks below manufacturing, in which about one-third of the employable males work. Only when manufacturing is divided into its diverse components does agriculture stand as the state's single most important industry. But since Wisconsin agriculture is preponderantly dairying, it is not too far off the mark to treat farming in general, unlike manufacturing, as a single industry. There are other agricultural products, but dairy products are undoubtedly the most important. Wisconsin is the nation's leading producer of milk and of a great variety of cheeses. There are some other special characteristics of Wisconsin agriculture. The state has fewer very large farms and fewer very small farms than the nation as a whole, and the family-type farm remains the standard Wisconsin unit.[14] Neither the ranch nor the truck-garden operation is typical. As might be expected with medium-sized units, there is a much lower farm tenancy rate in Wisconsin (14 per cent) than in the nation as a whole (24 per cent). The significance of an agricultural economy based on owner-operated units is apparent, and it is being qualified only in degree as the number of such units declines while the acreage of a "family-type" farm tends to increase with more highly mechanized operations. The day when Wisconsin farmers will no longer be a numerous and therefore influential group of property owners is still far-off despite their long-term continuing decrease in numbers.

By national standards, Wisconsin farmers are prosperous. The level-of-living index of farm operators in Wisconsin is 155 compared to 134 for all farm operators in the United States.[15] This prosperity is not uniform but is considerably more consistent in the southern than in the central and northern counties. While the fairly conservative Farm Bureau Federation is the strongest interest-group organization in the more populous south, the Farmers Union has a large membership particularly in the marginal agricultural sections of the northwest. However, there is no exact correspondence between farm wealth and membership in a particular farm organization.

Turning to nonagricultural establishments, it is plain that Wisconsin has a higher proportion of manufacturing employment within this general category than is true of the United States as a whole. On the other hand, there are very few miners in Wisconsin and a somewhat smaller percentage of service and government employees than there is in the rest of the country.[16] In manufacturing alone, which accounts for 43 per cent of the state's total nonagricultural employees, by far the largest single industry is the manufacture of machinery, even apart from the electrical machinery category. This is the case whether measured by number of employees or by value added by manufacture. Other large manufacturing industries, in order of their number of employees, are food and kindred products, electrical machinery, fabricated metal products, transportation equipment, and paper and allied products. No single industry, even machinery, accounts for as much as one-fifth of the total manufacturing employment.[17] Thus there is a considerable diversity instead of a one-product dominance like that of automobile manufacturing in Michigan. This also means that there is no single union like the United Automobile Workers with an overwhelmingly large membership. Wisconsin unions, like Wisconsin industries, tend to be diverse.

Except for the manufacture of food products and for a resort business based on lakes and woods, the state provides no great natural resources for economic expansion. Consciousness of this lack, along with an awareness of some locational disadvantage in being off the main east-west transportation arteries, adds urgency to the concern, usual enough in most states, to maintain and attract industrial development, particularly by advancing the St. Lawrence Seaway. Such a development appears necessary if Wisconsin is to provide employment for the continuing movement of population from the state's farms. Already, as noted, there is a net migration out of the state, which indicates the marginal status of Wisconsin as a growing industrial state.

INSTITUTIONAL FORMS

General election laws

Many Wisconsin election provisions are statutory rather than constitutional, and in principle readily subject to change. In fact, however, there have been no major changes in Wisconsin's election statutes since early in this century, and it is fair to view their provisions as very well established. Those of direct concern here relate to partisan elections, and it is only necessary to note that there are separate nonpartisan spring elections of all judges, municipal councils and administrators, town officials, and county board members. For partisan ballots in the fall, this leaves the eight county administrative officers (sheriff, district attorney, clerk, register of deeds, clerk of circuit court, treasurer, coroner, and surveyor), state legislators, U.S. representatives and senators, and the state's constitutional officers (governor, lieutenant governor, secretary of state, attorney general, and treasurer). All of these positions are listed on a single ballot, headed by the governor and the other state constitutional officers, but they are separated from the presidential ballot.[18] Since the party-column form is used, it is possible to vote a straight ticket, from governor through county officers, either by checking a single party circle at the top of a paper ballot or by pulling a single lever of a voting machine. Only in a presidential year does the straight-ticket voter have to make more than one motion.

This last feature may just possibly be less permanent than some other aspects of the election statutes. In addition to the usual proposals to eliminate the party-column ballot and thus straight-ticket voting altogether, there has been a recent suggestion to print only one ballot, and that a party-column ballot, in presidential years so that one could vote a straight ticket from president through county officers by a single check mark. Although this change was presented in 1957 in the form of a legislative bill, it received only slight support. Among other objections, there was a feeling among the numerous Republican officeholders, especially at the county level, that in many years their party's presidential candidate might make their ticket less rather than more attractive.

Returning to the rudiments of present laws, all partisan elections are for two-year terms except those for the state Senate (four years) and of course for the U.S. Senate. There is no legal limitation on the number of times a governor, other state constitutional officers, or legislators may be re-elected. At the county level, only the sheriff is limited, and he to no more than two consecutive terms. Elections are held in even-numbered years, and with every second state election thus coinciding with a presidential election it is evident that, except for the separate ballots previously noted, no effort has been made to insulate Wisconsin politics from national voting trends in the way attempted by states which, like New York or New Jersey, schedule gubernatorial elections only in nonpresidential years.

Wisconsin laws do not make minority-party and independent candidacies impossible. If a party cannot qualify for a column on the state ballot by virtue of the fact that one of its candidates for state-wide office in the previous election polled one per cent of the vote for that office, it may still obtain a place by a petition signed by electors in ten counties equal to one-sixth of the vote cast in each of those counties in the last gubernatorial election. Independents wanting a place on the general election ballot must obtain 5,000 signatures if they are candidates for state-wide offices, and reasonable percentages of voters if running for legislative and county offices. While these provisions have been used, their chief importance in recent years has been in the case of county-level candidates desiring to run as independents when dissatisfied with a given party nomination. In the past, minority parties played a considerable role. That they do not now do so appears to be caused by factors other than the election laws. Mainly by custom rather than statute, general election contests are between Republicans and Democrats.

In places over 5,000 and in Milwaukee County generally, the registration of voters is required. Registration is permanent in the usual way; that is, once registered, if one does not move from a given precinct or neglect to vote for two years, his name remains on the rolls. Registration is optional, and unusual, in places smaller than 5,000. In no instance does registration include the voter's party affiliation or preference.

One general feature of Wisconsin election provisions deserves further comment. That is the exclusion of municipal officers and councils from partisan election. Whether this be good or bad public policy is not to be discussed here, although it might be noted that the distinction which Wisconsin makes between municipal and county officers, both administrative in function, is hard to justify on policy grounds. What ought to be stressed, however, because of its political consequences is that the choice especially of big-city mayors on a nonpartisan ballot makes such positions less likely steps in a political career leading, for instance, to the governorship than might otherwise be the case. Although it is true that the legally nonpartisan elections in large Wisconsin cities do often become quasi-party contests, the absence of the regularized party-selection process is nevertheless significant. Often a mayoralty candidate finds it expedient and congenial to avoid party identification informally as well as formally, and so he becomes generally unavailable as a subsequent party nominee for other offices.

Party nominations

While the state's laws with respect to general elections have no sharply distinguishing feature, those affecting party nominations assuredly do. All nominations for all offices are by direct primary, and at the primary election (held only two months before the general election) the voter may decide which party's candidates he wants to help nominate.[19] There is no record, by registration or affirmation, of the voter's commitment to one party or another. He may simply make up his mind while in the primary-election voting booth which party's nominations he wants to try to influence. He is given two or more party ballots (or the equivalent choice on a voting machine), and he can vote on any one—but only one at a given primary—without indicating to an election official which one he voted. Accordingly the Wisconsin voter can be a Republican at a September primary, a Democrat at the following November general election, and then a Republican again at the primary two years later.

To be sure, this open primary is not quite so free and easy as Washington's arrangement, which allows the voter to move from one party's ballot to another at the same primary in order to choose his favorites on different tickets provided, of course, that they are running for different offices. But Wisconsin's primary is a good deal looser than is usual in the United States. In the more frequently employed closed primary, an effort is made to obtain some advance commitment, either by registration or affirmation, of the voter's party preference so that he is eligible to receive only one party's primary ballot. Proposals to change Wisconsin from an open to a closed primary state have been made, particularly by Republicans troubled by Democratic intrusions in their primaries, but the chances for change have not been great. The institution of the open primary in Wisconsin dates from 1906, and by now the political habits associated with it are deeply fixed. To many Wisconsin citizens, it would seem undemocratic to be asked to identify publicly with a party as a prerequisite for primary voting, and to restrict oneself in advance to a given party's ballot would seem a foolish deprivation of the opportunity to vote for (or against) an important personality on another ticket. In particular, voters in Wisconsin are accustomed to taking a hand in county-level primaries of the local majority party even though they may be attached to another party at the state and national levels.

The openness of Wisconsin's primary is not lessened by any statutory recognition of party organizational endorsement of candidates. Although, in a manner to be discussed later, both Republicans and Democrats have unofficial organizations (in addition to statutory parties for certain formal purposes) and the Republican organization does endorse candidates, such endorsement can in no way be indicated on the ballot as it is in some states (by an asterisk or other sign) where the statutory party endorses in an officially recognized convention. Nor, looked at from another point of view, is there any legal way to prevent a Democrat, for instance, from becoming a candidate in a Republican primary. Not only would he get his name on the ballot, but there would be no indication on that ballot of his Democratic connection. However, unlike the California cross-filing arrangement, a candidate cannot enter more than one party's primary at a given election.

Getting on the primary ballot is a fairly simple matter of obtaining signatures on nomination papers. The number of signatures required is not unreasonably high. For example, a candidate for state-wide office nomination by a party that polled over 200,000 votes in the last gubernatorial election needs an aggregate of 3,000 signatures distributed so as to include at least one per cent of the voters of his party in each of six counties. Candidates for other than state-wide office nominations need correspondingly fewer signatures. A small but not necessarily unimportant provision calls for printing individual candidate names on the ballot in a rotating order so that the same name will not be at the top of the list in each precinct.

Executive and legislative offices

The governor's position is limited by a number of factors, not all deriving directly from constitutional arrangements. Prominent among these factors are the two-year term of office and the election, rather than the appointment, of the attorney general, secretary of state, and treasurer (as well as the lieutenant governor). The usual provisions for government-by-commission also constitute limitations on the governor's authority although he has the authority to appoint commission members subject to confirmation by the state Senate. Generally his appointive power is limited to top-level positions, but it has occasional political importance within this narrow sphere.

On the composition of the state legislature, the Wisconsin constitution is explicit in certain highly consequential ways. In providing the usual bicameral system, the constitution specified that the Assembly should have no more than 100 members and the Senate no more than one-third the members of the

Assembly. Thus the figures of 100 and 33, reached early in the state's history, have long been regarded as fixed. Similarly established from the start is the requirement that there be only single-member districts in both houses. Of special significance, as it has recently turned out, is the constitutional direction that after each U.S. Census both houses should be redistricted "according to the number of inhabitants." While this provision did not prevent many years, really decades, of delay in a redistricting that would give urban areas some of the old rural seats, it did mean that any permanent rural legislative majority could be achieved only by changing the constitution. Unlike the situation in many states, the original Wisconsin constitution had not established either house on the basis of area representation. Thus in the 1950's, when pressure for a long postponed reapportionment of some kind became politically irresistible, the legislature first approved an equitable plan entirely in accord with the constitutional mandate for representation based on population, and then attempted to supersede this plan with one based on a constitutional amendment allowing one house to be apportioned according to an area principle. This new constitutional principle was first disapproved and then approved by popular referendum, but the state supreme court nullified it on technical grounds and thus restored the first and population-based reapportionment.[20] Admittedly, it was this judicial intervention which was finally decisive, but the legislature's awkward procedure, caused largely by the constitutional directive, provided the opportunity for the court ruling.

Whatever the cause, Wisconsin since 1954 has been unusual among American states in its achievement of equitable legislative reapportionment in accordance with population.[21] Or, to put it plainly, urban Democrats are fairly represented in both houses. There is no deliberate underrepresentation of urban areas which in many northern states causes the Democrats to be a permanent minority in at least one house and so without the opportunity ever to control all branches of a state government. That kind of "frustration of party," as Key calls it,[22] is now absent in Wisconsin, and it seems likely to remain so. Equitable urban representation, though achieved as recently as 1954, is not easily reversed by a legislature elected from the new districts. For some time into the future, area apportionment is a dead issue in Wisconsin.

Campaign regulations

Most of Wisconsin's elaborate and detailed statutory regulations of political campaigns can be ignored because, as is true elsewhere, such regulations are largely ineffective. This is especially so with respect to the severe legal limits placed on expenditures by candidates and by formal party organizations.[23] The principal consequence of these limits is to force any large-scale expenditures to be made by voluntary committees, either in behalf of particular candidates (i.e., by a Jones-for-Governor committee) or in behalf of a party ticket (i.e., by a Republican or Democratic voluntary organization instead of by the legally established party committees). In the latter instance, the consequence of the legal limits does have a special significance. The virtual substitution of voluntary (or extralegal) party agencies for the usual statute-prescribed apparatus, precinct committeeman through state central committee, is partly a symptom of Wisconsin's hyperregulation. The behavior of the statutory agencies is so stringently regulated, particularly in the matter of campaign expenditures, that candidates and party leaders have found it expedient to abandon these agencies except for fulfilling some formal obligations imposed by law, such as providing election-booth workers and replacing nominated party candidates who have died between the primary and the general election. The voluntary extralegal parties, on the other hand, have assumed most political chores, and they must be discussed later at some length.

A few other aspects of the state's regulation of campaign expenditures deserve note. The legal limit on a candidate's own financial contribution is low enough so that it could prevent a rich candidate from spending as much in his own cause as he would like, but since rich candidates are likely to have rich relatives the handicap is not serious. The state's ban on contributions by corporations is similarly narrow in its effectiveness; corporation executives are prevented only from contributing in behalf of their companies, not from contributing as individuals. A newly instituted (1955) ban on union contributions, paralleling for state campaigns the ban imposed by the Taft-Hartley Act for national campaigns, is of possibly greater consequence since it is more awkward for union leaders than for corporation executives to contribute large amounts personally. However, unions may continue spending money from their treasuries on political activity within their own organizations, and they may, in effect, also contribute to outside political activity if money is collected separately from union dues. All that is restricted is expenditure from union dues on a general political campaign.

Wisconsin does require a fairly detailed reporting of campaign contributions and expenditures by all candidates, committees, and organizations. The report is supposed to include the names of all contributors of five dollars or more, but even when this provision is observed it is doubtful whether contributors of large amounts are effectively discouraged by the fact that their contributions will thus become a matter of public record. In the absence of any legal ceiling on contributions by noncandidates, there are often generous donations. Despite some political criticism of the financing of campaigns by a relatively few large contributors, the state, like the country generally, seems to regard large contributions as a fact of political life.

One important respect in which Wisconsin practice differs from that of many states is in the very limited role of patronage in the political process. Aside from the handful of high-level positions, mainly filled by gubernatorial appointment, the state government is staffed—and has been largely so for half a century—by a well-developed civil service recruited by competitive examinations. It is impossible for an individual candidate or a party to build a political organization based on state patronage appointments or on the prospect of such appointments. Civil service is of such long standing and so taken for granted that a party would run great political risks if it sought to introduce large-scale patronage. The prohibition of political activity by civil service employees is accordingly a meaningful regulation. It should be added that the absence of patronage is not seriously qualified by practices at the county level, where the number of courthouse positions filled by political appointment is too small to be of broad significance. About all Wisconsin has by way of possible rewards for large numbers of party adherents are polling-booth jobs on election days, and the occasional nature of this employment severely limits its appeal. More important is whatever federal patronage may be administered through state parties.

Whether the virtual elimination of significant state patronage indicates a relatively "clean" political environment in other respects may be questioned. Obviously this matter is highly subjective, and the fact that in recent decades there has been no scandal involving corruption of state officials is not conclusive evidence. Wisconsin citizens do, it is true, tend to speak and write of their government as honest by comparison with that of other states, but this may be no more than local pride or overemphasis on the wickedness of neighboring Illinois. The elimination of patronage is not synonymous with the elimination of corruption, and even if outright corruption is put to one side there are bound to be interests, other than aspiring appointees, hoping for governmental favors, perhaps in the form of contracts, if the right people are elected to office. By all the usual statutes, Wisconsin has sought to protect itself against such practices, and it ought to be said that there is widespread confidence that this protection is generally effective. At least, the state's expectations are high with respect to the moral level of its politics. This attitude is of a piece with a fairly moral tone in other respects. Although Wisconsin's liquor laws are liberal, there is a statutory ban against gambling that effectively prohibits race-track operations as well as slot machines.

Antiorganizational bias

Partly as a way of summarizing the import of the state's institutional forms, it is useful to stress the strong legal bias against any organized political apparatus. There has been a deliberate effort, dating at least from the progressive era of the early years of this century, to limit the intercession of any agency between the voter and his elected officials. This goes beyond the Jacksonian democratic tradition, also perpetuated in the state, of having many administrative officials elected rather than appointed. What Wisconsin, certainly as much as any other state, has also tried to do is to have these officials nominated as well as elected by voters as individuals. This is the meaning of the open primary and of the ban imposed on the legal nomination of candidates by organized parties. Wisconsin law treats parties as though they might pervert the real will of the voters. The resemblance of this outlook to the famous view of Jean Jacques Rousseau is probably accidental, but the basic assumption is surely similar. Like Rousseau's underlying belief, that on which Wisconsin's institutions rests is that the citizen can choose most truly when he acts as an individual member of the whole community and not as a member of any group within that community. In one sense, this is a most highly individualistic political theory, and usually framed for a rather small and simple society in which citizens may be presumed to know each other. Furthermore, the theory ignores the influence which nonparty groups may exert if parties are rendered ineffective.

Here it is worth pointing out that some of Wisconsin's more individualistic democratic institutions were, in fact, developed in an environment somewhat simpler, and certainly much more rural, than that described earlier in this chapter. In particular, the reactions against party organizations, so typical of the progressivism of 1900, seem to reflect a confidence in the independent and more or less self-informed citizen that is more in keeping with the image of a rural midwest, populated by farmers and storekeepers, than with a contemporary urban community where everyone cannot know everyone else, or even know everyone running for office. The fact that much of Wisconsin's antiorganizational legislation did not come until 1900, when urbanization was well under way, does not negate the rural identification. On the contrary, it is possible to view the individualistic bias of progressivism as an attempt to develop political institutions consistent with an older and preferred order that was already threatened or even partially destroyed.

At any rate, Wisconsin law and custom have preserved a strong individualist political tradition. Increased urbanization has not eliminated the heavily personal character of the state's politics. Especially at the local level, but to a lesser extent at the state level too, primary campaigns tend to be based on individual records and individual personalities. To be running without organizational support, or even against the organization, is considered a political virtue. No doubt, this is far from unusual in other American states. The most that ought to be said relative to Wisconsin is that the custom seems especially widespread and firmly established.

CHAPTER III

A two-party Wisconsin?

FOR the United States, the familiar Anglo-American belief in two-party competition generally amounts only to a preference over the one-party system. In practice, the multiparty pattern is rarely an alternative. Party competition is conceived as affording the voter a choice between the "ins" of one party and the "outs" of *the* other. However, the one-party situation does prevail, in varying degrees, in many states at the same time as there is genuine two-party competition for control of Congress and the Presidency. On this score, it is the South which naturally attracts most attention, and political scientists have devoted considerable effort to explaining the reasons for the South's deviation from the two-party pattern, to deploring some of the consequences, and to searching for signs of change.[1] Among the deplorable consequences, students have emphasized that southern politics, conducted without the benefit of interparty rivalry, often become chaotically factional and thus fail to provide the voter with a clear-cut choice between recognizable organizations and policies.

Less systematic attention has been given to nonsouthern deviations from the two-party system. Partly this is because such deviations are by no means so pronounced or so durable as those of the South. Indeed the one-party variation of the North (and the border states) is really a distinct phenomenon. It has been accorded a name, "modified one-party type," by Ranney and Kendall, who place it in between the two-party and the one-party systems in their threefold classification of states.[2] Admittedly, this classification is rough although a refinement relative to the usual simple division into one-party and two-party systems. Quite properly, Ranney and Kendall call for detailed examinations of each state party pattern so as to allow for careful comparison between states.

It is to this task that the present chapter on Wisconsin's party system is devoted. What should be noted at the outset is that Ranney and Kendall have classified Wisconsin among the two-party states, rather than among the modified one-party states, and that this classification will be qualified, for the past, in light of what seem to have been Wisconsin's "normally Republican" politics. Actually Ranney and Kendall were able to classify Wisconsin as a two-party state only because they included (not unreasonably) the victories of third-party Progressives in their count of total second-party victories.[3] However, this addition of Progressive to Democratic wins could be misleading with respect to non-Republican strength both before and after the six election years (1934–1944) of the separate Progressive party. Before 1934 and again in 1946, the pattern of the Progressives, particularly of their La Follette family leadership, was to compete within the Republican party. The consequent intraparty rivalry is crucially different, for purposes of the present analysis, from a normative two-party pattern.

Altogether Wisconsin's party system is difficult to classify. Its status varies greatly in relation to various criteria of classification. In presidential voting, of the 1914–1952 period (the Ranney-Kendall period), Wisconsin displays a two-party pattern (five Republican wins and four Democratic, plus the elder La Follette's capture of the state's electoral vote in 1924). But in the 21 gubernatorial elections of the same period, Republicans won all but four (one Democratic and three Progressive). And over all the years from 1861 through 1956, Republican governors were chosen in 42 out of 49 elections. Then there is the 1934–1944 period which, if considered alone, indicates a short-lived and rather unstable three-party pattern in state elections.

Broadly speaking, however, Wisconsin is here conceived as moving from what looked like a modified one-party system, prevalent in the earlier decades of the twentieth century, toward a two-party pattern. This is chiefly according to the criterion of state rather than national elections. It is in state contests that there is something novel, for twentieth-century Wisconsin, in the postwar development of politics along the lines of Republican-Democratic competition. But the local novelty of the contemporary situation is not the only reason for studying its development. The nature of the change in Wisconsin politics ought to be relevant to a general understanding of influences, like that of the direct primary, on party patterns elsewhere in the United States. In particular, the Wisconsin experience may illuminate some of the problems involved in the establishment of a fullblown two-party system in a state with a strong one-party background. It is logical, then, to begin with a discussion of that background in Wisconsin.

POLITICAL BACKGROUND

In the post-Civil War decades of the nineteenth century, Wisconsin's dominant Republicanism broadly resembled that of most north-central states.[4] Opposition of a substantial sort still came from the Democratic party. Until 1896 the Democratic vote for governor never dropped below 40 per cent of the two-party total, and most of the time it hovered about 46 or 47 per cent. Furthermore the Democrats won the state's presidential votes once (for Grover Cleveland), and the governorship three times in the twenty elections from 1859 through 1898. In each of these Democratic gubernatorial victories, there had been specific and unusually sharp grievances against Republican administrations.[5] Although the results were not such as to change the long-term majority position of the Republicans, it is significant that at least through the nineteenth century the Democratic party did serve as the political agency for an occasionally effective mobilization of opposition to the "ins." Wisconsin could then claim a virtue of the two-party system: voters did have an organized alternative to a generally dominant majority party.[6]

During these late nineteenth-century decades, and persisting many decades later, much of Wisconsin's two-party division of the vote derived from circumstances usually described as "traditional." As elsewhere among northern voters, the Civil War had equated Republicanism with patriotism and respectability.

This was especially true in the Wisconsin counties settled by Yankees from New England and upstate New York. Here identification with the cause of the Union often confirmed a preference for Republicans as the heirs of the Whigs, or perhaps of the Know-Nothings or even the abolitionists. The liquor issue also served to solidify the support which the temperance-minded, native American Protestant accorded the Republican party.

Conversely, the traditional Democratic support was heavily derived from those outside the scheme of values represented by the Yankee conscience. Both German and Irish immigrants found the Democratic party relatively congenial. Numerically the German element was more important, and even into the early part of the twentieth century, particularly until World War I, the rural counties settled mainly by Germans (Protestant or Catholic) turned out Democratic votes more or less in the pattern established by 1860.[7] The city of Milwaukee also provided a substantial Democratic following of a similar traditional sort, although the city's pattern came to be modified by Socialist influences. It goes almost without saying that the Wisconsin Democratic party was not a vehicle designed either for economic protest or for political reform. By any standard, it was at least as conservative as the Republican party even though attracting many relatively recent immigrants who were economically and otherwise insecure in the American community. The late nineteenth-century Wisconsin Democrats were about as progressive as Tammany Hall at the same period (and much less effective). The point is of importance, since the stereotype of the state's Democrats as the party of rum and Romanism, if not of rebellion, became a fixture in the political consciousness of many Wisconsin citizens.

That such an opposition party should become weaker rather than stronger in the first years of the twentieth century would not have been surprising in any circumstances. But there is little doubt that the decline of the Democrats as an effective second party owed much to the presence in Republican politics of the first Robert M. La Follette and his progressive movement. Of course, much of what a realistic and ambitious politician thought of the relative prospects of the two major parties is indicated by the fact that La Follette himself, in the 1880's, chose to be a Republican and then continued to campaign as a Republican despite two failures before 1900 to gain the party convention's nomination for governor. At any rate, the overwhelming success of La Follette in finally capturing the Republican party in 1900, and in dominating it during much of the next quarter-century, rendered nearly impossible any vitalization of the Wisconsin Democrats as a liberal opposition. The state's considerable zeal for reform, both in terms of ideas and individuals, was almost entirely channeled into the Republican party. In fact, the Democratic party became a residual agency not only for its own traditionalists, but occasionally for conservative Republican voters who preferred Democratic candidates to La Follette. Only briefly and abortively, under the external stimulus of Wilsonian liberalism, did Wisconsin Democrats show any signs of changing their historical position.

In the whole period from 1900 to 1932 Wisconsin politics were fought largely within the Republican party. Never in those years did the Democrats win the governorship, and never except in the early Wilsonian years (when a Democrat won a U.S. senatorship) did they have any serious chance of gaining power in the state. Only in the three-way presidential contest of 1912 did the Democratic party win Wisconsin's electoral votes. At times the Democrats seemed to be little more than a minor party; in 1922 the Democratic candidate for governor received only 12 per cent of the two-party vote, and in 1926 only 17 per cent. The Socialist party seemed almost as strong just after World War I, when Socialists were continuing to elect Milwaukee's mayor and were also electing a Milwaukee congressman and casting almost one-sixth of the vote in state-wide contests.

During this period of Republican supremacy, the form of the intraparty contest is of principal concern. The direct primary was instituted in 1906 under the inspiration of the elder La Follette, then serving his third term as governor.[8] Subsequently the struggle between La Follette progressives and anti-La Follette conservatives, or stalwarts, was not for party convention delegates but for voters. In view of the openness of the primary, the relevant voters were practically the electorate-at-large, and not a closely defined Republican electorate. Any voter wishing to participate in the only serious election contest simply chose the Republican primary ballot. Although it can be argued that the state's very one-party situation as of 1906 made the primary especially appropriate (as in the South), nevertheless the opportunity of choice which the primary subsequently afforded the voters tended to obviate any need or desire for a two-party system. Much of the time the Wisconsin electorate was confronted with two alternative slates of candidates, one progressive and the other conservative, seeking the Republican nomination for the state's executive and legislative offices. Both Republican factions had leadership cadres resembling those of separate parties elsewhere in the United States. Insofar as this bifactionalism prevailed in Republican primary contests, Wisconsin escaped the chaotic personal and locally based rivalries which have been found to characterize much of the one-party South.[9]

However, bifactionalism did not always clearly prevail in Wisconsin's Republican primary. At times the progressive-conservative line was loosely drawn, and at other times one faction failed to achieve a consensus with respect to its candidates. Furthermore, in accord with the spirit of the reformers who instituted the primary, it was relatively easy for an individual to get on the ballot. And it turned out to be possible occasionally for a popular personality (or for a personality with a well-known political name) to win the Republican nomination for state-wide office even without organized factional support. Multiple candidacies were common (Table III-A), and, because the primary law contained no provision for a southern-style runoff between the two highest candidates, the successful Republican nominee was often the choice of only a minority of the party's primary voters. In fact, from 1912 through 1946 Republican gubernatorial candidates won their party's nomination without gaining majorities in eight of the eighteen primaries. And in Republican senatorial primaries of the same period, mere plurality victories were scored in five out of the twelve contests.[10] Primary contests for other state-wide offices were in much this same pattern. But despite multiple candidacies and plurality victories, it is probably fair to say that bifactionalism sufficiently characterized the Republican primary so that the alternatives were more often defined in progressive-conservative terms than they were in many two-party states between 1906 and the mid-1930's.

Wisconsin voters concentrated on the Republican primary in the same manner, if not in the same degree, as have southern voters on the Democratic primary. It was ordinarily the decisive election. In the most extreme instances, 1922 and 1930, the Republican primary vote for governor actually exceeded the total votes cast for gubernatorial candidates of all parties in the subsequent general election.[11] Generally, however, Wisconsin did not thus resemble the familiar southern pattern even in other off-year (nonpresidential) elections.[12] It is more appropriate to measure Wisconsin's one-party system by some more frequent indication than that provided by the two unusual instances when the Republican primary vote actually exceeded the all-party general election total. There were many other years when there was simply an excess of Republican primary votes over Republican votes in the general election—which is an indication of a less drastic but nevertheless pronounced one-party attraction. This occurred (that is, the Republican total decreased in absolute terms from the primary to the general election) in eight of the fourteen gubernatorial election years from 1906 through 1932, the real heyday of Wisconsin's one-party system (col. 4 of Table 2). Except in two of these eight years (1922 and 1930, as already noted), the all-party total increased from primary to general election. Thus, in light of the Republican decrease at the same time, one of two things (or perhaps both) must have happened. Non-Republican voters who had not bothered with the primary might have voted instead of some Republican voters who, having cast primary ballots, saw no point in the general election. Or, more probably, since the total vote increased between the two elections, a fair number of voters in the Republican primary must subsequently have voted Democratic in the general election.

At any rate, in every biennial election year from 1906 through 1956 (except in the special circumstances of 1912 and 1938),[13] the Republican percentage of the total primary vote exceeded the Republican percentage of the total general election vote (compare cols. 2 and 3 of Table 2). This decrease

Table 2

WISCONSIN REPUBLICAN GUBERNATORIAL PRIMARY VOTE
IN RELATION TO OTHER VOTES CAST, 1906–1956

Year	Rep. Primary Vote as % of Total Primary Vote	Rep. General Election Vote as % of Total General Election Vote	Rep. Primary Vote as % of Rep. Vote in General Election
1906	83	64	93
1908	77	59	66
1910	75	59	118
1912	45	52	45
1914	59	53	88
1916	76	58	76
1918	78	58	121
1920	87	60	103
1922	93	88	136
1924	91	56	104
1926	94	70	131
1928	90	58	94
1930	96	70	169
1932	82	44	156
1934	26	19	86
1936	34	30	46
1938	43	56	42
1940	56	41	66
1942	68	38	91
1944	70	53	45
1946	86	60	73
1948	80	55	70
1950	71	54	70
1952	80	63	69
1954	59	52	55
1956	60	52	49

in proportion of the vote cast is even more striking, because of its persistence, than the previously noted absolute decrease (which occurred eight times). But whether measured in absolute or relative terms, the point in calling attention to the Republican decrease from primary to general election is to stress that party's strength, not weakness. The almost consistently better Republican showing in the primary is an index to Wisconsin's one-party tendency.

That tendency persisted in spite of the strong counterforce exerted by national politics. By no means was Wisconsin unaffected by the broad politico-economic movements which for substantial periods of the twentieth century made the national leadership of the Democratic party a vehicle for social protest. In fact, because of agrarian discontent with farm prices and, more importantly in recent years, a steady growth of large-scale manufacturing and urbanization, Wisconsin has been so obviously affected by contemporary trends that the growth of the more usual two-party system might have been expected at least in the 1930's. That such a system did not develop is especially striking in light of Wisconsin's voting record beginning in 1932. In the five presidential elections of the Roosevelt-Truman era, only once (1944) did Wisconsin fail to give its electoral votes to the Democratic candidate. In 1932 Roosevelt won 67 per cent of Wisconsin's major-party presidential vote, and in 1936 the figure was 68 per cent.[14] Both of these percentages were well above Roosevelt's national proportion (59 per cent in 1932 and 62 per cent in 1936). Yet these overwhelming Democratic presidential voting records failed to vitalize the Wisconsin Democratic party (Figure 3). The traditional residuum of state Democrats was ill-suited, and not entirely willing, to become the Wisconsin wing of the New Deal, and the opportunity afforded by Rooseveltian triumphs was largely wasted. Only in 1932, in the wake of the national landslide, did Wisconsin Democrats win state-wide offices (including the governorship and U.S. senatorship), and thereafter Democratic percentages declined continuously in each gubernatorial election of the 1930's.

The inadequacies of Wisconsin's archaic Democratic organization were not solely responsible for the failure to establish a two-party system in the 1930's. Prepared to take advantage of the absence of liberal Democrats in a liberal period were the two sons of Robert M. La Follette—Robert, Jr., an incumbent Republican U.S. senator, and Philip, who had been a Republican governor from 1931 to 1933.[15] In 1934, when the Senator was to seek re-election and Philip wanted to regain the governorship, it was plain enough that the Republican ticket, just then, was not the place for a family accustomed to winning office. Nor, for different reasons, was the Democratic party inviting to the La Follettes. For one thing, old-line Democrats

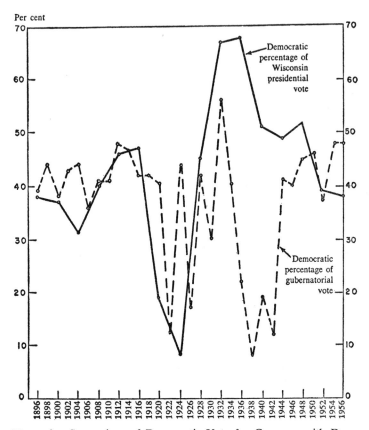

Figure 3.—Comparison of Democratic Vote for Governor with Democratic Vote for President in Wisconsin, 1896–1956

(Per cent Democratic is of two-party vote except for presidential elections of 1912 and 1924 and the gubernatorial elections of 1934–1944, when per cent Democratic is of three-party vote.)

were now officeholders, and they coupled a conservative antipathy for progressivism to an understandable desire to keep the La Follettes from taking over the jobs which Democrats had so recently and surprisingly won. Secondly, the La Follettes could hardly avoid the impression that the Democratic label, whatever its value in the early 1930's, was traditionally disreputable in Wisconsin and might well be so again. Thirdly, in addition to estimating the liabilities of the state Democratic

party, the La Follettes could also have calculated that the time
was finally ripe to begin in Wisconsin what would become a
new national party.[16]

Whatever the reasoning, in 1934 the La Follettes took almost
all of their following out of the Republican party and into a
separate Progressive organization. They managed to secure
Roosevelt's blessing for the La Follette senatorial candidacy,
and at least a kind of national Democratic neutrality with respect to the gubernatorial contest. National patronage arrangements came, in part, to benefit the Progressives. They competed
successfully for Wisconsin's pro-Roosevelt vote, winning the
governorship in 1934 and 1936 in addition to holding their
Senate seat in 1934. Also in these halcyon days of the New
Deal the Progressives were well represented in the state's congressional delegation and in the state legislature. By 1936 the
Democrats were reduced to a decidedly third-party status, and
in 1938 they almost lost their separate identity when their
regularly chosen gubernatorial candidate withdrew in favor of
the successful Republican opponent of Philip La Follette. The
formal Democratic substitute polled only eight per cent of the
total 1938 vote for governor, as many traditional Democrats
cast Republican ballots. Such liberal Democrats as there were
had little choice, at least temporarily, except to vote Progressive
in state politics.

This anomalous situation, in which Wisconsin politics were
so out of line with national politics, did not endure. The Progressive alliance with the national Democratic administration
cracked under the combined force of Philip La Follette's
abortive (and somewhat comic) national third party of 1938
and the subsequent division between the internationalist Roosevelt and the isolationist La Follettes. Then the Progressives
were so unfortunate as to have the governor they elected in
1942 (against the inept Republican incumbent) die before he
could assume office. In 1944 they proved unable to maintain,
without a well-known candidate and in the atmosphere of a
presidential campaign, their status as a major party. For the
first time since 1934 the Democratic candidate for governor
ran second.

It could be said that the three-party system was ended, but it is not so clear that it ever really existed. In only one of the six gubernatorial elections during the life of the Progressive party did each of the three parties receive more than 20 per cent of the vote. And in two elections one party failed to win as much as ten per cent. The system was more like that of two and one-half parties. First one and then another of the three parties was reduced to a plainly minor role as the votes tended to divide mainly between the "ins" and one set of "outs." In the end, it was the originally victorious Progressives, without fixed national identification, who dissolved.

IMPORT FOR THE POSTWAR PERIOD

Although the La Follettes returned to their father's Republican mansion in 1946 (which, exactly contrary to 1934, looked like a year when only on the Republican ticket could one get elected in Wisconsin), the result was not the fullfledged re-establishment of the pre-1932 pattern of Republican primary contests. Instead, at least after 1946, there arose a two-party rivalry which needs to be explored in some detail. However, before doing so it is worth while summarizing the import of Wisconsin's recent political history. The years from 1932 to the end of World War II now appear transitional as far as the party system is concerned. It is true that once the popular peak of the New Deal was past, Wisconsin's Republicanism reasserted its dominance. But during the 1930's an appreciable realignment took place as Progressives found it expedient, at least temporarily, to leave the Republican party, and many conservative Democrats to leave the Democratic party. Consequently the Republican party was left to the conservatives, who have not since lost their control, and the Democratic party became more than ever a narrow group of traditionalists and national patronage-seekers (southern Republican style). If the Republican party was now fundamentally conservative, the Democratic party was nearly a vacuum, say at the start of World War II, in terms of ideology and personnel. Unless progressivism could re-establish itself as a strong force within the Republican party, the Democratic party would be the obviously convenient vehicle for Wisconsin liberals to take over. At least this would be the case so long as the national Democratic party stood to the left of the Republicans.

The last point deserves emphasis. The position of the national parties always exerted some influence on Wisconsin politics. In this respect, a one-party state of the Wisconsin type has been less thoroughly immunized from external forces than a southern state. Not only was the 1932 Roosevelt landslide accompanied by the brief elevation of Democrats to Wisconsin offices, but generally in this century the Democratic vote for governor tended to be higher in presidential years than in off years (and, of course, markedly higher in the good Democratic presidential years). In the period 1896–1954, the mean average Democratic gubernatorial percentage was 39.9 for presidential years, and 33.7 for off years. Wisconsin Democrats, campaigning for state offices, were uniformly associated with a more popular national ticket in every presidential year from 1928 through 1952 (Figure 3). On the other hand, from 1896 through 1924 there had been only one presidential election (1916) when the Democratic gubernatorial percentage was lower than the Democratic presidential percentage in Wisconsin. The difference between the 1896–1924 pattern and the 1928–1952 pattern probably reflects the decreasing strength of Wisconsin Democratic traditionalism at the very time that an increasingly attractive Democratic party, of New Dealish cast, won national elections. A third pattern may be reflected in the 1956 results, when the Democratic candidate for governor ran far ahead of Adlai Stevenson.

It is the 1928–1952 pattern—the product of earlier decades of state Democratic decline—which meets the political scientist's expectancy. As Key puts it, the state vote for a minority party tends to lag behind the national vote, and a state that is Republican nationally over a long period will probably be more Republican in state affairs.[17] On this count, Wisconsin surely conformed to type. Throughout the twentieth century, before and after 1928, state political battles were usually fought within the Republican party in defiance of the fact that, along with much of the rest of the country, Wisconsin voters made national decisions within the two-party context. The movement since

1946 toward a state two-party system was counter to the customs of most voters and most officeholders.[18] Certainly it is more reasonable to describe the situation in this way than to say that the Wisconsin electorate was accidentally deprived of a two-party system for fifty years and was simply waiting for a return to normalcy. Rather the state's political background has been such as to provide a largely alien environment for the development of a stable two-party pattern.

INCIPIENT TWO-PARTY POLITICS

Whether Wisconsin politics of the postwar years fell into a stable two-party pattern is hardly a settled question. Despite substantial Democratic gubernatorial percentages after 1948, and a high of 48.5 per cent in 1954, the Republicans certainly remained dominant by the measure of state officeholding. Democrats failed, through 1956, to elect a governor, and they won only one of the other four state elective offices—and that one (the attorney-generalship) for a single term when Republican voters had unusually strong cause for deserting their nonregular candidate. Similarly Democratic candidates for U.S. senator were regularly defeated until the surprise and decisive victory of William Proxmire in the special election of August, 1957. Whether this victory was largely personal and peculiar to the circumstances, or whether it was the beginning of a new pattern in party voting, could not be decided except in subsequent regular election years.

Congressional officeholding presents a similar if less complete Republican pattern. The Democrats did reach a postwar high in 1954 and again in 1956 when they elected three of the state's ten congressmen. Two of the three were from Milwaukee County, where one district is marginal and the other is a heavily Polish populated working-class area of large Democratic majorities. The third Democratic congressman was returned from the largely rural ninth district in northwestern Wisconsin, where agricultural prosperity is well below the state average.[19] Aside from these three districts, Democrats, even in their better years, were serious contenders in no more than two of the remaining seven districts. Not only did the Republicans hold all seven pretty securely in the first six postwar election years, but they also regularly won the ninth district until 1953 [20] and captured the marginal Milwaukee district in 1946, 1950, and 1952.

Generally speaking, Republican dominance of the Wisconsin congressional delegation seemed stronger than the party's hold on the governorship. This is illustrated by the fact that in 1954 and 1956 the percentage of the total state congressional vote cast for Republican candidates exceeded the percentage of the total gubernatorial vote cast for the victorious Republican candidates (Table III-B). The source of this differential is clearer when it is seen that the Republican congressional percentage was markedly above the Republican gubernatorial percentage in the eight congressional districts outside Milwaukee, and below the gubernatorial percentage in Milwaukee where the winning Democratic congressional candidates ran far ahead of their party's state ticket.

More fully indicative of the continued Republican dominance through 1956 than either the state-wide or congressional elections is the county-office pattern.[21] Here the durability of a one-party tradition is most evident and probably most significant. Wisconsin Republicanism is strongest at its base, or roots, in the county courthouses, as measured by the election in each of Wisconsin's 71 counties of the eight county office-holders on the same partisan ballots and at the same time as choices are made for state offices. The results even in the relatively good Democratic year of 1954 were 77 per cent Republican. That is, out of 542 offices in which there was at least one candidate,[22] Republicans won 472 and Democrats only 70. And for many of the 542 offices there was no Democratic candidate. The victor in the Republican primary simply won the general election without contest. Altogether, in 1954, in 13 of the 71 counties there were no Democratic candidates for any of the eight offices, and in 10 counties the Democrats had candidates for only one county office.

Since the calculations above count small counties equally with large ones, over-all Democratic weakness at the county level is more significantly revealed by the percentages of the two-party vote cast in 1954 for the two most prominent county offices, sheriff and district attorney. As shown in Table III-C, the Democratic percentage of the state total for each office is well below the 48.5 per cent mark reached by the party's gubernatorial candidate, and is especially low in district attorney contests. In the latter case, the Democratic percentage is also substantially lower than the percentages (ranging from 44 to 47) polled by the little-known Democratic candidates for the state-wide offices of lieutenant governor, secretary of state, treasurer, and attorney general. Without much doubt, the particularly low Democratic poll for the district attorney posts is the most serious of the several indications of Democratic weakness at the county level. There were more gaps in Democratic candidacies for district attorney than in those for sheriff, and this reflects the inability of the Democratic party to attract enough of the ambitious lawyers who ordinarily provide the political ability and the middle-class respectability which make a party a going concern locally. Even when district attorney candidates have come forward, in many areas they lacked the status to compete seriously against their Republican competition. Thus the Republicanism of Wisconsin communities often perpetuated itself.

Of course, this is to speak only of those counties in which Republicans customarily occupied near-monopolistic political positions. But that category included most counties. Milwaukee was by far the largest of the several exceptions, and it is notable that there the Democratic candidates for sheriff and district attorney (as well as the Democratic candidates for Congress) have run well ahead of the Democratic state ticket. Consequently when Milwaukee County votes (in 1954) are subtracted from the state totals for sheriff and district attorney, then the Democratic percentages of the remaining totals (the outstate vote) fall much below the corresponding Republican percentages and well behind the outstate gubernatorial Democratic percentage (Table III-C). In general terms, then, it is plain that the majority party in a given area enjoyed a larger margin in county contests than in state-wide contests. This is an extension of Key's observation, referred to earlier, that a state which is Republican nationally over a long period will probably be more Republican in state affairs. Most Wisconsin counties, long Republican in state affairs, remained more Republican in county affairs. And consistently enough in principle if not in direction, a few counties (of which Milwaukee is a prime example), now regularly Democratic in state as in national affairs, were correspondingly more heavily Democratic in county affairs. The significant point is that the postwar Democratic counties were not only few among the total of 71 counties, but they contained something less than half of the state's voting population.

However, there were some indications of Democratic growth which counter the picture of Republican preponderance in officeholding. The very fact that Milwaukee County became regularly Democratic after World War II is significant. Earlier, despite Rooseveltian landslides, the county had Republican and Progressive county officeholders in addition to some Democrats. The next most conspicuous of the newly regular Democratic counties was Dane, containing the capital (Madison) and the state's second largest population (but still less than one-fifth of Milwaukee County's). Dane County offices were largely captured by Democrats in 1948, and this former home of the La Follettes and stronghold of the Progressives has remained Democratic since that time. An index to Dane County's postwar party habits is provided by the Democratic retention of the courthouse in 1952 despite county majorities for the Republican presidential and gubernatorial candidates. With Milwaukee, Dane, and a few other (but by no means all) industrial counties as their principal base, Wisconsin Democrats became serious contenders for state power.

Although 1948 is the date of the organization of the contemporary state-wide Democratic party, it is probably correct for the observer of the movement toward a two-party pattern to look to 1944 as a turning point. In that year the Democratic candidate for governor was Daniel Hoan, the former Socialist mayor of Milwaukee, and his 41 per cent of the three-party vote marked the emergence of the Democrats as a New Dealish party and as the major opposition, instead of the Progressives, to Republican incumbents. Also in 1944 the Democratic candidate for U.S. senator, a liberal Milwaukee congressman named Howard McMurray, polled an even higher percentage than Hoan's. Although in 1946 the Democrats declined in relative strength, this seems to have been the result of temporary factors. For one thing, 1946 was nationally a very good Republican year. And, secondly, the return of the La Follettes to the Republican fold brought an increase in Republican strength that could not necessarily be counted on for the future.

As a matter of fact, the main event of Wisconsin politics in 1946 was the defeat of Senator La Follette in the Republican primary by Joseph McCarthy. This defeat, in many ways fortuitous,[23] was decisive for Wisconsin's future party history. Never again did a La Follette campaign for state-wide office. But if Senator La Follette had succeeded in capturing the Republican nomination and thus, undoubtedly in 1946, retained his Senate seat, there would have been a major officeholder capable of attracting, as in times past, much of Wisconsin's liberal and labor vote into the Republican party. There might even have been a revival of the bifactionalism which traditionally prevailed in the Republican primary.

In retrospect, such an eventuality seems unreal. What La Follette was trying to do in 1946 (and almost succeeded in doing) now looks anomalous. Here was a liberal, according to virtually any standard established by domestic issues, who sought the label of the party which was the more conservative of the two parties nationally and even more decidedly so, as it turned out, in Wisconsin. It is hard to believe that La Follette's postwar Republicanism could have been any happier than Senator Wayne Morse's. Nevertheless what La Follette wanted was very much in the traditional pattern of Wisconsin politics. It is by no means evident that he could have returned to the Senate as a Democrat even in some more favorable year after 1946. At least, the choice La Follette made in 1946 represented his best chance for success. As it was, he might have attracted enough Democratic voters into the Republican primary to give him the nomination if the La Follette isolationist record had not afforded the Democratic party some reason for urging its voters to stay in their own primary. To this extent, it is fair to say that national politics obtruded so as to prevent the full liberal mobilization which the La Follettes had formerly commanded when they contested Republican primaries. And what a La Follette failed to achieve proved far beyond the reach of any progressive Republican who bore a less famous name.[24]

By 1948 Wisconsin's customary bifactionalism—of progressive against conservative—was transferred from the Republican primary to a two-party general election contest. It was in 1948 that liberal Democrats, including many younger ex-followers of the La Follettes, established the state-wide Democratic Organizing Committee (later called the Democratic Party of Wisconsin) and began recruiting a membership which in most counties assumed Democratic leadership in place of the largely moribund statutory party. Here the Democrats were following a Republican lead. For over twenty years, the regular or conservative Republicans had found it convenient to focus their activities, not in the statutory party, but in the Republican Voluntary Committee (later called the Republican Party of Wisconsin). In the 1920's, the Voluntary Committee was necessary because the La Follettes controlled the statutory organization, but later (and to some extent always) the unofficial vehicle was useful as a means of avoiding the financial limitations imposed by law on the official party. Similarly the Democrats, when they wanted in 1948 to build a liberal-oriented organization, chose the unofficial form in order to have a less closely regulated kind of party.[25]

The two so-called voluntary organizations, Republican and Democratic, became for all practical purposes the only organized political movements in postwar Wisconsin politics. Progressivism, as such, had no separate identity. La Follette followers, if they were to remain active politically, usually had to choose between Republican and Democratic organizations. Which they chose is a fascinating problem. To some extent, age played a part. The older Progressive leaders tended to become Republicans, and the younger more often Democrats. Sometimes, however, the determining factor may have related to officeholding. Those Progressives who occupied county or legislative positions in 1946 might well have associated their tenure in office with the resumption of the Republican label. In this respect, and more generally too, there was a variation according to place and section of the state. Urban Progressives, especially in the larger metropolitan centers where labor was highly organized and already voting Democratic, had good reason to select the Democratic label. Rural and small-town Progressives, on the other hand, in most cases made a readier adjustment to local voting habits by becoming Republicans. This is not to suggest that calculations of political advantage were the only motivations of the old Progressives. Ideological preferences played a part. Just as some found the New Deal cast and the union labor orientation of the Democrats to be congenial, so there were others among the La Follette following who did not identify their progressivism with post-Rooseveltian urban politics. And just as some of the younger Progressives found the internationalism of the Roosevelt and Truman administrations an attractive feature, so there were many others, nurtured in La Follette isolationism, who looked to Robert Taft's Republican party as their last hope for getting the United States out of Europe.

Although not much statistical light can be cast on what happened to the apparently ubiquitous individual Progressives, there is some point in observing the county-by-county relation of the postwar Democratic vote and the Progressive vote of former years.[26] The index used for the Democratic vote is an average of the percentages of the two-party vote, in each of the 71 counties, for gubernatorial candidates in the four elections of 1948–1954. For Progressive strength, the index is an average of percentages received, in each county, by Progressive candidates for governor and U.S. senator in nine contests from 1934 through 1946.[27] All nine of these elections, except for La Follette's Republican primary contest of 1946, involved third-party Progressives (whose percentages are therefore of the three-party total). The coefficient of correlation turned out to be .50—high enough to indicate some relation between old Progressive and recent Democratic strength but not so close a relation as might have been expected on the assumption that today's Democrats occupy the leftward place in Wisconsin's political spectrum formerly filled by the Progressives.[28] Interestingly the coefficient was slightly higher (.56) when the Democratic gubernatorial percentages in the peak year of 1954, taken alone, were correlated with the Progressive percentages.

From the scatter diagrams made at the same time as these correlation coefficients were calculated, it appears that most of the deviation which precluded a closer association between the old Progressive vote and the later Democratic one can be explained by the fact that (with some exceptions) Progressives were relatively stronger in rural and mixed urban-rural counties and relatively weaker in metropolitan centers. Thus it was mainly in rural counties that postwar Democratic percentages, despite some gains in 1954, were not so high as to correspond to the general relation (as indicated by the line of regression). And it is principally in urban counties that the Democratic percentages were greater than those of the general relation.

Although these differences in respective party strength are appreciable, there remains enough association between current Democratic and old Progressive patterns to indicate the likelihood of some continuity in voting behavior from one party to the other. Ideologically, this likelihood seems greater than does a continuity from the former traditional Democratic party to the postwar Fair Deal Democrats. In fact, postwar Democrats ran especially poorly in some of the counties which the old Democratic party, even into the mid-1930's, used to carry. A simple measure is provided by a comparison of the 1948–1954 gubernatorial results, by counties, with the traditional alignments of counties listed in the older and useful study of Wisconsin politics by Gosnell and Cohen.[29] Of the top fifteen Democratic counties of the postwar years, only four had been among the top fifteen traditional Democratic counties. And, more significantly, four of the fifteen traditional Democratic counties were among the top fifteen Republican counties in 1948–1954!

Generally what happened is that the postwar Democrats lost certain counties of prosperous farms and small manufacturing cities, mainly in the well-populated Fox River Valley and in the adjacent area to the south. Here the party's strength had rested on old historical foundations, and always before 1934 the Democratic vote in these areas was above the party's state average. On the other hand, from 1948 to 1956 the Democratic vote here was below the state average.[30] This change reflects the general dominance of postwar Republicans in almost all of the more prosperous agricultural counties as well as in most counties characterized by small and medium-sized manufacturing cities. Democratic rural majorities were, through 1956, generally confined to counties in the northern cutover region and in the marginal areas of the northwest. And urban Democratic majorities were, in this period, mainly limited to the few areas which are metropolitan centers or parts of such centers: Milwaukee, Dane County (Madison), Douglas County (Superior), and Racine and Kenosha counties.

In most respects, this alignment seems similar to the contemporary division of the two-party vote in most northern states. The socioeconomic line between Republicans and Democrats was, however, probably modified by party traditions as well as by ethnic and religious factors. And in Wisconsin it was the Republican tradition which weighed heavily. The Democrats, as observed, no longer had much of what had been their older traditional following. Unlike the Republicans, the postwar Democratic party was relatively new and necessarily untraditional in its appeal to Wisconsin voters.

Nevertheless, Wisconsin's postwar two-party rivalry became relatively clear-cut and apparently viable. Only once during the postwar years did the Democratic gubernatorial percentage drop below 40 (in 1952). Further indication of the apparent permanence of the Democratic opposition comes from the fact that the party's gubernatorial percentage actually rose both times between presidential years and off years, 1948 to 1950 and 1952 to 1954 (Figure 3). Not too much should be made of this phenomenon because, having occurred only twice, it might be the result of various factors unrelated to long-term Democratic strength. Still the relatively strong showing in the off years is striking enough to be noticed in the case of a party whose hopes of victory in the past rested on national coattail riding. That the coattail riding era had ended was best illustrated by the way in which the gubernatorial candidate in 1956, William Proxmire, maintained virtually intact his 1954 percentage despite the much poorer showing of the party's 1956 presidential candidate (Figure 3). More emphatic still was Proxmire's actual victory in the special Senate election of 1957.

Any development of the two-party system, in which Democrats were at least serious rivals of Republican officeholders, might be expected to coincide with a decline in the formerly overwhelming electoral attention focussed on the Republican primary. The record, as reflected in Table 2, furnishes partial evidence of such a decline. When the 1948–1956 period is compared with that of the one-party days of 1920–1932, the Republican primary vote is seen to have diminished both as a percentage of the total primary vote and as a percentage of the Republican general election vote. The significance of this difference is blurred, in the tabular presentation, because the Republican primary vote was also low during most of the three-party years of 1934–1944. More convincing perhaps as an indication of the Republican primary's changed status is the absence of gubernatorial contests in the three election years from 1952 through 1956 (Table III-A). To account for this new situation, two apparent causes exist. The first, already discussed, is the disappearance of an organized intraparty progressive opposition to the conservative regulars. The second and related cause (to be discussed in Chapter Five) is the extent to which the regular organization (the Republican Party of Wisconsin) has been able to discourage substantial opposition to the candidates it endorses in the primary. On this latter point, it must be noted that the Republican organization failed thus to discourage substantial opposition only when it was challenging an incumbent (or, in one case, a man who was the son of a long-time incumbent). On such occasions, and particularly in 1956 when the party sought to defeat Senator Wiley, the Republican primary attracted some of the central attention that it did in the old days.

In ordinary circumstances, however, major state-wide competition appears to have been transferred from the Republican primary, even though the Republican nomination remained very much worth having.[31] Challenging in a state-wide primary contest the regular Republican choice, especially if also an incumbent, appeared too difficult now that organized progressivism ceased to be an internal Republican force. The best illustration is provided by the futile efforts of a vigorous and able antiorganizational Republican, Len Schmitt. First, in 1950, he ran against the nonincumbent but endorsed Republican candidate for governor, Walter Kohler, and was defeated two to one. Then, in 1952, Schmitt challenged Senator McCarthy's bid for his second Republican nomination, and despite the dramatic nature of his cause Schmitt lost by a margin of five to two. This showing was particularly poor compared to that of McCarthy's Democratic opponent, Thomas Fairchild, in the general election. Fairchild, running far ahead of his party's presidential and gubernatorial candidates, polled (in a much larger turnout) three times as many votes as had Schmitt and received about 46 per cent of the total senatorial ballots.[32] These 1952 results did much to show that the primary had become a less likely place to defeat a regular Republican incumbent.

SUMMARY

Compared to its experience during the rest of the twentieth century, Wisconsin in the postwar years surely came closer to two-party politics as ordinarily conceived. Serious competition for Republican officeholders at the state-wide level came more regularly from Democrats in general elections than from primary opponents. However, through 1956, the state had not yet reaped the presumed advantages of party alternation in officeholding. Until the special senatorial election of 1957, Democratic candidates had not won major state-wide elections even though they had occasionally been serious contenders. Their majorities in metropolitan centers and in marginal farming areas were not sufficient to overcome traditional Republican strength. The special bases of this strength are to be analyzed in some detail in the next chapter.

Here it remains only to stress the importance of the maintenance of this Republican voting tradition throughout the postwar decade. It helps to explain, in particular, the much-debated question of how a state that elected the elder La Follette could subsequently have elected McCarthy. Both, it must be remembered, were Republicans, and this may be urged as an important common element of their electoral appeal along with personal dynamism and foreign policy positions. The record shows that Wisconsin voters were at least as consistent in electing Republicans as they were in electing anti-internationalists.

CHAPTER IV

Size of place and the two-party vote

THE division of the vote between Republicans and Democrats in Wisconsin's new two-party environment of the postwar decade has already been discussed in general socioeconomic terms. However, this division can be further amplified by the classification of election returns according to the size of place in which votes were cast. In particular, such classification serves to explain the nature of the Republican majority that was maintained in Wisconsin at least through 1956, and thus in years in which state-wide Democratic victories were scored in neighboring states. A clue to Wisconsin's political experience in this respect is to be found in the description, in Chapter Two, of the state's heavier-than-usual concentration of urban population in small and medium-sized cities and the correspondingly smaller metropolitan proportion. What the present chapter seeks especially is to show the relation between this population pattern and the division of the two-party vote.

Whether such a relation—for instance, that voters in small cities are less Democratic than voters in larger cities—would prevail elsewhere than in Wisconsin is another question and one that cannot be answered here. In some states, small cities may be mill towns or mining centers and more heavily Democratic than larger commercial cities. However, the possibilities of comparison are interesting, and it is hoped that whatever emerges here concerning the relation of size of place to the division of the two-party vote may be tested in other states, both where the population pattern is similar and where it is different. Comparison seems most appropriate in other relatively urban and industrial states of the North, particularly of the Great Lakes area. As already indicated, postwar competition between the Wisconsin parties broadly resembles the socioeconomic alignment of such states. The traditional Republican background of Wisconsin also resembles that of other states in the same region, differing mainly and importantly in the relative newness in Wisconsin of serious Democratic opposition.

No more serious methodological problem is encountered in this kind of study than that of classifying and then laboriously tabulating election returns according to the size of place in which votes were cast. The hazards of ecological correlation are largely avoided. On the other hand, the tedium of the labor required has caused this inquiry to be confined to the four gubernatorial elections of 1948–1954 and to the special senatorial election of 1957. (The most obvious gap is the 1956 gubernatorial contest, where the apparent similarity to the 1954 results did not seem to justify the additional tabulating chore.) Most of the analysis is based on the four governorship elections. Some argument might be made about the suitability of these elections as a representation of Wisconsin's two-party vote, but broadly speaking the contests for the governorship between 1948 and 1954 seem to have been more nearly clearcut as Republican-Democratic competition than any other group of state elections during the same period. Gubernatorial elections, occurring every two years, tend to be regarded by the parties themselves as reasonably representative of their respective strengths. The governor is elected at the head of a ticket which includes all other state and county candidates. On occasion, of course, a given gubernatorial candidate may run ahead of or behind his party's candidates for other major offices. For example, in 1948 the successful Republican gubernatorial candidate won many more Wisconsin votes than did presidential candidate Thomas Dewey, who lost the state. And in 1952 the Republican gubernatorial candidate, as well as the Republican presidential candidate, ran well ahead of Joseph McCarthy, the party's candidate for re-election to the U.S. Senate.

Yet such results do not necessarily run counter to the idea that gubernatorial contests are fair tests of party strength. It is at least as likely that presidential or senatorial showings are deviant from the "normal" two-party division of the vote. More or less in support of this view is that none of the 1948–1954 gubernatorial candidates, Republican or Democratic, possessed the kind of public personality which at the time dominated political attention.[1] No doubt, candidate personality played some part in the results of the governorship races, as in other contests, but there is no basis for thinking that it played so unusual a part as to destroy the usefulness of the gubernatorial election data for present purposes. And it happens that there is a strong positive reason for using the gubernatorial results: they are readily available in state records, precinct by precinct, for each of the four elections.

Most of the data of this study are presented in Tables 3 and 4. The breakdown, according to size of place, is the same for both and also for Table 5. The explanatory notes attached to the first table apply to the others as well. Table 3 is the heart of the study. It indicates the division of the two-party vote, expressed as Democratic percentages of the total (which percentages may, of course, be subtracted from 100 to derive Republican percentages). Table 4 is designed to show merely the portion of the state's total two-party vote that was cast in each of the size categories. Table 5 relates only to the special senatorial election of 1957.

The differentiation among communities, it will be observed, is considerably more elaborate than a simple urban-rural division. The state's single large metropolitan area—the only one which rises much above the 100,000 mark—is separated from all lesser urban centers. Below this metropolitan level, there are established five other categories which the U.S. Census defines as urban in character (that is, places with populations over 2,500). Within the rural classification which remains, there is a fourfold division; two, by size, for incorporated places, and two for townships (or "towns," as they are legally referred to in Wisconsin). The separation between townships, as will be explained later, is designed so that areas populated predominantly by farmers may be considered apart from townships which have become quasi-urban.

With this breakdown by size of place, three of the following

Table 3

DEMOCRATIC PERCENTAGE OF TWO-PARTY
GUBERNATORIAL VOTE, 1948–1954

Geographical unit	1948	1950	1952	1954
Wisconsin state-wide	44.9	46.4	37.4	48.5
Milwaukee County	53.7	54.1	51.1	55.7
Urbanized areas and cities over 50,000 except Milwaukee	54.4	59.3	46.1	56.0
Cities of 25,000 to 50,000	43.9	43.8	35.2	45.0
Cities of 10,000 to 25,000	45.0	46.8	35.7	45.5
Cities of 5,000 to 10,000	35.9	39.2	25.8	37.0
Cities of 2,500 to 5,000	38.0	40.2	28.4	38.4
Cities and villages of 1,000 to 2,500	37.2	40.3	28.4	38.4
Cities and villages under 1,000	36.3	38.6	26.2	37.1
Townships with less than 50 per cent farm population	42.1	42.5	34.9	46.9
Townships with more than 50 per cent farm population	39.0	42.3	27.3	49.3

Milwaukee County, used as a unit because of convenience in tabulating election returns, almost coincides with the Milwaukee urbanized area as defined by the U.S. Census.

Urbanized areas outside Milwaukee are (according to the 1950 Census) Madison and Racine plus that part of the Duluth-Superior area which is in Wisconsin. Two cities, Green Bay and Kenosha, are over 50,000 and are here included with the three urbanized areas (none of which is much above the 100,000 mark).

Cities, villages, or townships within Milwaukee County are counted *only* in that category. Also places within urbanized areas are included in that category except that a few townships, with less than 50 per cent of their population within an urbanized area, are excluded from such areas in order to count their election results along with other townships. At any rate, no place has its election returns counted more than once.

Unincorporated places are not counted as such, but their election returns are tabulated as part of the townships within which they are located.

The term "township" is employed in accord with customary American usage even though in Wisconsin the legal term is "town" for what is a township in most other states.

Sources

U.S. Bureau of the Census, *U.S. Census of Population: 1950,* Vol. 1, *Number of Inhabitants,* Chapter 49, "Wisconsin" (Washington, D.C.: U.S. Government Printing Office, 1951).

Wisconsin Legislative Reference Library, *Wisconsin Blue Book* (Madison, editions of 1950, 1952, 1954, and 1956). Data in Table 5 on the 1957 senatorial election are derived directly from the election returns filed with the Wisconsin secretary of state.

Wisconsin Crop and Livestock Reporting Service, *County Agricultural Series* (Madison: U.S. Department of Agriculture and Wisconsin State Department of Agriculture, 1952–1955). Series contains farm population and total population for each township.

general propositions are to be examined in light of the 1948–1954 election data and the fourth proposition by comparing the senatorial election data of 1957:

1) Democratic voting in the largest cities has not been duplicated in medium-sized cities.

2) Republican voting has been especially strong in small cities and villages.

3) Farm voting has been more changeable than the voting behavior of most of the state.

4) General voting characteristics of size-of-place categories in Republican years would also prevail in case of a party overturn.

Answers to these hypothetical propositions cannot, because of the limitations of the data, be persuasive beyond the period of Wisconsin politics here under consideration.

THE DIFFERENCE BETWEEN LARGE AND MEDIUM-SIZED CITIES

Immediately apparent in each of the four elections of Table 3 is the sharp drop in the Democratic percentage from the first two categories to the third—that is, from places above 50,000 to those below that figure. To be sure, there is some difference, particularly in 1952, between Milwaukee County, on the one hand, and the urbanized areas and cities over 50,000, on the other. But this difference is not nearly so striking as the regular drop of over ten percentage points between the latter and the 25,000–50,000 category. Since there is no such drop between the 25,000–50,000 class and the next lower 10,000–25,000 class, it appears that the "medium-sized" cities of these two categories (altogether there are 22 cities so classified) vote in a significantly different pattern from that of the state's large cities.

There is nothing so unusual about this finding. It conforms, in general, to the results of other studies.[2] The only possible novelty lies in establishing the breaking point between the category above 50,000 and that below 50,000, rather than between the single metropolitan center of Milwaukee and the next largest places (the biggest of which, the Madison urbanized area, has only 110,111 people). But obviously, since there are

Table 4

TOTAL TWO-PARTY GUBERNATORIAL VOTE, 1948–1954

Geographical unit	1948		1950		1952		1954	
	Total	%	Total	%	Total	%	Total	%
Wisconsin state-wide	1,243,336	99.8	1,130,968	99.9	1,611,015	100.1	1,156,904	100.0
Milwaukee County	328,739	26.4	288,028	25.5	429,437	26.7	292,176	25.3
Urbanized areas and cities over 50,000, exc. Milwaukee	129,052	10.4	121,471	10.7	160,687	10.0	126,634	10.9
Cities of 25,000 to 50,000	116,008	9.3	107,768	9.5	149,885	9.3	114,565	9.9
Cities of 10,000 to 25,000	70,203	5.6	66,714	5.9	88,162	5.5	66,265	5.7
Cities of 5,000 to 10,000	57,599	4.6	54,496	4.8	72,512	4.5	53,949	4.7
Cities of 2,500 to 5,000	66,300	5.3	64,107	5.7	85,738	5.3	61,192	5.3
Cities and villages of 1,000 to 2,500	65,426	5.3	63,639	5.6	85,327	5.3	63,962	5.5
Cities and villages under 1,000	62,512	5.0	59,277	5.2	80,619	5.0	58,717	5.1
Townships with less than 50% farm population	93,555	7.5	87,998	7.8	135,277	8.4	94,171	8.1
Townships with more than 50% farm population	253,942	20.4	217,470	19.2	323,361	20.1	-225,273	19.5

only five Wisconsin places in the category of urbanized areas and cities over 50,000, it may be purely fortuitous that the voting pattern resembles that of Milwaukee County instead of that of the category of cities just below 50,000. For instance, the results would have been altered somewhat if heavily Democratic Superior, which alone is considerably below the 50,000 mark, had not been classified among the state's urbanized areas (the U.S. Census so defines the city as part of the Duluth-Superior area). It is well, then, to appreciate that the level of 50,000 hardly represents a firmly fixed breaking point, and also that it is derived from a comparison of voting by groups of cities and not from a rank order of cities according to their separate election results. What can be said is that at *about* the 50,000 level there has been an appreciable drop in the Democratic percentage, and that this level corresponds with what is roughly understood to be the line between large and medium-sized cities rather than the line between a great metropolis and all other cities.

A likely question is whether the higher Democratic vote in larger cities compared to medium-sized cities is related to the type of employment in places of one size as opposed to places of the other size. More particularly, do the larger places have higher percentages of their population in what can be called "urban working-class" occupations? The prime difficulty in dealing with this question arises from the definition of "urban working-class." Counting within that class virtually all nonfarm manual workers seems too broad and general for purposes of comparing occupational patterns between large and medium-sized cities.[3] On the other hand, the elimination of certain kinds of manual workers is hard to achieve without being arbitrary. For want of a better ready measure, there appears to be some point in trying an index of employment in manufacturing— even though granting that employees in construction, mining, and transportation (to cite leading examples) are as likely to be unionized and to be working-class in their orientation as are employees in factories. Manufacturing at least has the virtues of simplicity and uniformity in definition.[4]

Taking those employed in manufacturing as a percentage of all those employed in each place and then deriving the mean

percentage for each size category, the following relevant figures
are obtained: 42.8 per cent engaged in manufacturing in Milwaukee County, only 34.0 per cent in the urbanized areas and
cities over 50,000, 40.0 per cent in the 25,000–50,000 category,
and 40.6 per cent in the 10,000–25,000 category.[5] Thus the
second category—the large cities which are so much more
Democratic than the medium-sized cities—actually have a considerably lower percentage of their employed workers engaged
in manufacturing. Especially noteworthy is that two of the urbanized areas, with consistently Democratic election results,
have particularly low manufacturing employment percentages.
One of these, Madison, has many white-collar workers in government and education, and only 16.7 per cent in manufacturing. The other, Superior, has a relatively large number of rail-
road and other transportation employees, but only 12.0 per
cent in manufacturing. On the other hand, two other Democratic voting places in the large-city category, namely Kenosha
and Racine, do have very high percentages of their employed
workers in manufacturing.

A similar absence of a relation, either positive or negative,
between manufacturing employment and the Democratic vote
is discovered by examining the data for individual cities within
the medium-sized category. Some places with higher-than-
average Democratic percentages have lower-than-average manufacturing percentages, and vice versa. The fact is that the index
of manufacturing employment cannot be significantly related
to the differential in the Democratic vote as between various
cities, even within the same size category, and so it is understandable that manufacturing employment fails to explain the
difference between the large-city vote and the medium-sized-
city vote.

In the absence of an explanation based on readily available
occupational data, it is useful to search for another alternative
to reliance simply on size to account for the difference in voting
as between large and medium-sized cities. One possible factor
is the number of foreign-born in each category. Given the usual
view of a positive relation between number of foreign-born and
Democratic voting, one would expect to find more foreign-born
in the larger cities. Based on the 1950 Census,[6] the percentages
of foreign-born of the total population are as follows:

Milwaukee County 9.6%
Urbanized areas and cities over
    50,000, except Milwaukee 8.5%
Cities of 25,000 to 50,000 .... 5.0%

Thus the expectation is borne out at least in the very general sense that the rank order of foreign-born coincides with the rank order of Democratic voting. Within the categories, however, there are some exceptions. Madison, among the Democratic urbanized areas, has only 4.6 per cent of its population foreign-born. And among the cities between 25,000 and 50,000 there are two which are below the 5 per cent foreign-born average in that category but which are as Democratic as most of the cities in the plus-50,000 class.

All that can be said, then, is that most of Wisconsin's cities between 25,000 and 50,000 have relatively fewer foreign-born than do most of the larger cities. The relation between this difference and the difference in the degree of Democratic voting could not, in any case, be settled conclusively except by careful interviewing of the foreign-born themselves. The more Democratic election returns of cities with larger percentages foreign-born do not establish that these cities are Democratic because of the presence of foreign-born, or that the foreign-born generally vote more heavily Democratic. And in this particular case the data do not so strikingly show a coincidence of foreign-born with Democratic voting as to establish even a very strong probability of connection. At most, the foreign-born figures indicate a small distinction in the general character of large as opposed to medium-sized Wisconsin cities.

This aspect of the character of Wisconsin's larger cities is not necessarily a function of size. Obviously there are in the United States many small and medium-sized cities with large foreign-born populations. The French Canadian populations of Maine's mill towns are cases in point. The foreign-born may have settled in various places for various reasons even though it be granted that there is, as in Wisconsin, some tendency to concentration in large cities.

The pertinent question at this point is whether there is anything about the very largeness of large cities which affects voting behavior, since it is not only in the present study that a correlation seems to exist.[7] Perhaps certain socioeconomic characteristics, other than foreign-born population, do almost inevitably go with increases in size. For example, in big cities it may be more likely that workers would live in a distinct neighborhood community, that factories would be larger and more effectively organized, and that more trained, capable, and politically conscious labor-Democratic leadership would be available. Such conditions, clearly associated with size of place, could well be decisive in obtaining Democratic votes in communities which, like most of those in Wisconsin, have been Republican historically. Where these conditions are absent, as they are even more obviously in the smaller than in the medium-sized cities analyzed here, Democratic electoral efforts suffer a relative handicap. Further discussion of this subject is especially relevant in the next section.

SMALL CITIES AND VILLAGES

In Table 3 the four categories of cities and villages ranging from 10,000 to under 1,000 all show roughly the same voting pattern. In any given election year, there is no appreciable difference between the four Democratic percentages. From election to election, of course, there is some variation, but the percentages in the four categories move up or down pretty much together. Therefore, it is reasonable for present purposes to treat these four separate sizes of the table as one group, under the label of "small cities and villages."

As a group, these places obviously constitute a Republican stronghold. Even in the better years for Democratic gubernatorial candidates, the Republicans polled about 60 per cent of the vote. And it is especially striking that in 1954 the Democrats did not increase their vote in the small cities and villages nearly as much as they did in the townships. Even the places under 1,000, though supposedly linked to the farm economy, did not respond in the same degree as did the townships to the Democratic critique of the Eisenhower-Benson farm program. Generally in 1954 the small cities and villages, while casting a higher Democratic vote than in 1952, nevertheless differed from the state-wide pattern in that they were more Republican than they had been in 1950. The apparent conservatism of these small Wisconsin places is not a negligible factor in determining state results. Altogether, as may be seen from Table 4, the cities and villages under 10,000 cast about one-fifth of the total two-party vote in Wisconsin. Unquestionably the Democratic bid for state office has been importantly affected by failure to attract more voters in small cities and villages.

Among individual places under 10,000, there is, as might be expected, considerable variation. For example, there is one mining community of 3,034 that regularly votes Democratic by a large margin, and there are a few other places, often factory towns, that are also exceptions to the generality of Republican voting in small cities. But there are some places where it is not unusual for the Republicans to have polled as high as 75 per cent or more of the vote. These variations are themselves interesting and perhaps explainable. However, it remains evident that when all of the small cities and villages, regardless of their character in other respects, are considered together, they display a more consistently Republican pattern than does the rest of the state.[8]

On the surface, the lower Democratic vote in small cities than in medium-sized cities might seem understandable in terms of the respective proportions of manufacturing employment. It is true that the mean percentage of employees engaged in manufacturing is considerably lower in the smaller places (29.3 per cent in cities of 5,000 to 10,000, and 30.8 per cent in cities of 2,500 to 5,000) than it is in the medium-sized cities (around 40 per cent, as already noted).[9] Nevertheless it is difficult to contend that manufacturing employment, as such, accounts for the difference in election results between medium-sized places and small places when, as previously pointed out, it could not account for the difference in election results between large cities and medium-sized cities.

A hypothetical explanation that at least has the merit of consistency in accounting for differences between cities of various sizes is that smaller places in general are likely to be more resistant than larger places to the kind of change in behavior which is implied by Democratic voting in Wisconsin's previously one-party Republican environment. Thus it may be suggested that places under 10,000 are less congenial to the growth of a new party than are places in the 10,000–50,000 category (and that the latter are less congenial than the still larger places over 50,000). What this suggestion involves is the belief that, apart from the nature of employment, voters in smaller places are more likely to be Republican—given, that is, an environment like Wisconsin's where politics has traditionally and prevailingly been Republican. As has been observed of dominant parties elsewhere, the Republican party of Wisconsin developed a "legitimate monopolistic political structure." [10] In many small cities and villages, and to a lesser extent in medium-sized places, Republicanism has remained the only approved vehicle for political action. Thus to become a Democrat is not only to join a minority; it is to become a social deviant. Such a break with tradition, in small cities and villages, must be even more difficult for potential leaders than for ordinary voters. What Key has written of small-town politics generally is neatly applicable:

> The strand of rural and small-town politics contributes a special color and tone to the American political system. Over considerable areas even yet such a politics is predominantly a one-party politics which is reflective of a highly integrated community life with a powerful capacity to induce conformity.[11]

In fact, the opposition may hardly be recognized locally, and at any rate probably not taken seriously in local elections. The "other party" remains an entity outside the particular community, however important it may be in national or even state affairs. Political issues do not so clearly divide the small city or village, and elections tend to be contested within a single party on the basis of rival personal claims either to popularity or administrative efficiency. The single approved political vehicle, which elsewhere may be the Democratic rather than the Republican party, almost automatically recruits the politicians.

What this view suggests is that reinforcing the political traditionalism of smaller places, that is, the Republicanism of Wisconsin's small cities and villages, is a relative homogeneity associated with their size. Class-consciousness is not entirely absent, but it is easy to believe that working-class consciousness is inhibited in smaller as compared with larger cities by the more readily available personal and social channels for communicating middle-class values. There is a greater opportunity for those values to pervade and dominate. The association of this phenomenon with size of place was discussed at some length in a well-known study of voting behavior in Elmira. Although in the case of this fairly large upstate New York city (in the 50,000–100,000 class) what was emphasized was that the working class did not vote so heavily Democratic as its counterpart in still larger cities, the import of the analysis was essentially the same as that stressed here. For Elmira, as for Wisconsin, it was possible to write of a class-conscious vote being "inhibited by the status of the dominant community ideology centered in the middle-class and its rural forebears." [12]

What may be added in relation to the Wisconsin data is the theory that the inhibiting factors are even stronger in smaller places than in those approaching the size of Elmira. A closer model may be "Jonesville," the midwestern city of just over 6,000 which was subjected to detailed analysis by a team of sociologists in the 1940's. In this community, part of a county in which there had been no Democratic courthouse officers in the twentieth century, the Republican party was the nearly all-sufficient political vehicle. The situation is summarized in the comment that it was "safer, from the standpoint of social and economic considerations, to vote Republican." [13]

A more generalized commentary on this aspect of voting behavior has been made by Duncan MacRae in his comparison of occupational composition and party vote in United States congressional districts. Among other things, he found that the association of low-income status (the "labor vote") with Democratic voting did not hold in rural districts as in urban districts. And, more significantly for purposes of the present study, MacRae concluded that the fact that there were relatively fewer persons in nonfarm labor occupations in the rural districts was not enough to account for the lower Democratic vote of such districts. As in the analysis of Wisconsin, some explanation other than that of the nature of employment had to be sought for the decrease in Democratic voting which coincided with diminishing degrees of urban living. The hypothesis which he suggested is that "where a high degree of community integration exists with a high degree of consensus on the prestige rankings in the community, political party identification will become assimilated to and be perpetuated by the value system." [14] This is essentially similar to the suggestion advanced with respect to Wisconsin's small cities and villages, which seem well qualified for the role of assimilating and perpetuating the state's Republican party identification.

A special factor that may be associated with this role is the age distribution of the population of small cities and villages. At least in the more rural of these places, as described in Chapter Two, there tends to be an older than average population because of the regular addition of retired farmers and the regular loss of ambitious younger people. Small cities and villages seldom have the economic advantages to attract residents representing new and different socio-political attitudes. The relatively static life of such communities is entirely compatible with attitudes of resentment against the politics of big cities, often identified as labor politics, and of resentment against bigness in general. While it is farfetched to think of the fairly prosperous businessmen of Wisconsin's small cities and villages as American Poujadists, they do, as the dominant elements of their communities, reflect a steady though moderate resistance to changes represented by high taxes, strong unionism, and foreign aid.

THE CHANGEABLE QUALITY OF THE FARM VOTE

The method of defining the farm vote is not perfect. Only those townships with more than 50 per cent of their populations actually living on farms are counted as contributing to the farm vote. To be sure, this eliminates some farmers, and also has the disadvantage of including some nonfarmers. But, all things considered, there appears to be no better dividing line than that of 50 per cent. The farm vote is still not purely farm in character, but it is reasonably close. Incidentally, what is left out, by way of townships with less than 50 per cent farm populations, is really unclassifiable in terms of the present analysis. The category contains too great a variety of places: residential suburban, industrial, resort, and mixed farm-suburban.

Nothing significant can be said concerning the nature of voting in so residual a grouping of places. The only purpose of having the grouping at all is to have some category in which to put the townships that were separated from those constituting a reasonable approximation of the farm vote.

What is most noticeable about the farm vote, as shown on the last line of Table 3, is the great fluctuation of the Democratic percentage from year to year. Not only did the Democratic vote of farm townships drop more sharply than that of any other place category in 1952, but it rose appreciably more in 1954.[15] The latter is ordinarily explained as an adverse electoral response to falling farm prices, particularly for dairy products, which appeared to coincide with the first two years of the Republican national administration. This explanation seems probable enough in light of the fact that the Republican gubernatorial candidate sought to defend the Eisenhower-Benson farm program, while the Democratic candidate spent a large share of his campaign in denouncing that program.

However much a change in farm prices seems to account for the vote in 1954, it does not really explain the results in 1952.[16] Then, when the Democratic percentage among farmers was especially low, the electoral behavior of farmers appeared un-related to agricultural prices—which, if they had been determining, would have prompted Democratic votes in support of then current farm prosperity. That the farmers, more than almost any other population group in Wisconsin, voted over-whelmingly Republican in 1952 must be attributed to other causes than those of agricultural economics. Of course, the Republican farm vote of 1952 did not represent a deviation, except perhaps in moderate degree, from custom. On the contrary, it may be assumed that heavy Republican voting is the traditional pattern among Wisconsin farmers as it is among residents of small cities and villages. However, Wisconsin farmers appear more likely to deviate, as in 1954, in response to a specific economic grievance. This seems also to have been the case in the early 1930's, when the state's farm vote was less Republican than that of small cities and villages.[17] It may be speculated either that farmers are more sensitive to economic change, or that they live in communities where deviations from

Republicanism are less restrained by accepted social values. Or, it should be added, both factors may be operative.

At any rate, even the temporary deviation of farmers from Republican voting preferences represents significantly different behavior from that of small cities and villages, and, for that matter, from that of medium-sized cities as well. If farmers are capable, in favorable circumstances, of being more Republican than any other group in the state, they can also, as in 1954, be much less Republican than voters in all groups of cities except those over 50,000. This volatility gives the farm vote an importance in Wisconsin politics beyond that indicated by mere numbers. In fact, the farm vote as here defined comprises less than one-fifth of the total state vote (Table 4). This proportion is not what is responsible for the lavish attention which politicians of both parties give to farmers and farm issues. Rather it is the demonstrated capacity of Wisconsin farmers for wholesale switching of party allegiance.

IMPACT OF STATE-WIDE DEMOCRATIC VICTORY

To learn whether the differences in voting according to size of place would hold in the event of a major change in party fortunes, it is worth while examining the data of the 1957 special senatorial election. Up to the time of this writing, William Proxmire's victory in that election was the only major Democratic triumph in the postwar years, and consequently the only means available to test the size-of-place analysis in the circumstances of party turnover. However, the special election has some drawbacks for this purpose. The total vote was only about two-thirds that of a regular November election in a non-presidential year, and the absence of a party ticket for lesser offices might have made the senatorial contest more personal than is usual at regular elections. Furthermore, by 1957 Proxmire had an especially large political acquaintanceship built during three successive gubernatorial races, the most recent in 1956 when he nearly duplicated his strong showing of 1954 despite the Eisenhower landslide. Still another, though minor, complicating factor was that independent candidates in the 1957 election polled nearly 3 per cent of the total vote, much of which one particular independent, a right-wing candidate, was thought to have taken from the Republican. Therefore, in calculating percentages of the two-party vote, Republican strength may be somewhat understated. More serious if less calculable as a possible understatement of Republican voting is that a bitter primary fight, in the absence of any organizational endorsement, left the losing non-Eisenhower Republicans unhappy about the nominee, former Governor Walter Kohler, and may have caused conservatives to stay at home at the subsequent election.

These peculiarities of the 1957 election are sufficient to make for caution in handling the results. Deliberately, then, the analysis of the special senatorial division of the two-party vote has been separated from the earlier presentation of the more "normal" gubernatorial results of 1948–1954, and the data arranged in Table 5 so as to leave the two preceding tables devoted solely to the four races for the governorship. Nevertheless, for convenience in interpretation, the 1954 data, which also appear in Tables 3 and 4, are included beside the 1957 data in Table 5. Comparison, even though qualified, can thus be made. Incidentally in choosing 1954 to go with 1957 the effect is to compare election contests between the same two candidates, Proxmire and Kohler.

From Table 5 it is apparent that in the general victory of the Democratic candidate the same broad distinctions, observed in the earlier analysis, remained as between size-of-place categories. In 1957, of course, the Democratic percentage was higher everywhere so that a few categories not previously carried now registered Democratic majorities. Yet the sharp drop-off in Democratic voting (at a given election) that was noted at the 50,000 population level still occurs, and so does that at the 10,000 level. Again too the lowest Democratic percentages—low enough so as to be short of majorities even in the 1957 state-wide landslide—were in the small cities and villages. Despite considerable weakening, these places remained Republican when the G.O.P. lost everywhere else. This is especially striking in comparison to the farm townships which, as in 1954, continued to poll much higher Democratic percentages than the small cities and villages. In fact, the farm town-

Table 5

COMPARISON OF THE 1957 SPECIAL SENATORIAL VOTE
WITH THE 1954 GUBERNATORIAL VOTE

Geographical unit	Dem. % of Two-party Vote		Two-party Vote			
			Total		Per cent	
	1954	1957	1954	1957	1954	1957
Wisconsin state-wide	48.5	58.2	1,156,904	748,916	100.	100.
Milwaukee County	55.7	62.2	292,176	218,065	25.3	29.1
Urbanized areas and cities over 50,000 except Milwaukee	56.0	61.8	126,634	90,390	10.9	12.1
Cities of 25,000 to 50,000	45.0	54.3	114,565	82,868	9.9	11.1
Cities of 10,000 to 25,000	45.5	55 0	66,265	44,440	5.7	5.9
Cities of 5,000 to 10,000	37.0	46.6	53,949	31,621	4.7	4.2
Cities of 2,500 to 5,000	38.4	46.1	61,192	33,216	5.3	4.4
Cities and villages of 1,000 to 2,500	38.4	48.4	63,962	35,904	5.5	4.8
Cities and villages under 1,000	37.1	48.7	58,717	34,767	5.1	4.6
Townships with less than 50 per cent farm population	46.9	58.9	94,171	55,625	8.1	7.4
Townships with more than 50 per cent farm population	49.3	64.0	225,273	122,020	19.5	16.4

ships in 1957 registered a higher Democratic percentage than did any other category, including normally Democratic Milwaukee County, and also the largest gain in Democratic percentage points, 1957 over 1954. Clearly the especially changeable quality of farm voting is thus confirmed even though the change from 1954 to 1957 is in the same direction as that from 1952 to 1954. If a farm revolt against the Eisenhower Administration was registered in 1954, it would seem to have been more definite in 1957.[18] Moreover, some of this revolt may have taken the form of nonvoting. The last columns of Table 5 indicate a sharper drop in the total two-party vote in farm townships than elsewhere, and particularly in relation to the larger (and Democratic) cities. The small cities and villages also polled lower proportions of the total state-wide two-party vote than in 1954.

SUMMARY

As they relate to the hypotheses with which this chapter began, the findings derived from Wisconsin gubernatorial elections of 1948–1954 and from the special senatorial election of 1957 are as follows:

1) Democratic majorities maintained in metropolitan Milwaukee County and in the category of other urbanized areas and cities over 50,000 were not generally extended to the class of cities below 50,000 during the years of Republican state-wide victories.

2) Republican majorities, while regular (1948–1954) in the category of medium-sized cities (10,000 to 50,000), were strongest and most persistent in the small cities and villages below 10,000.

3) Farm voting shifted more radically than the voting in any other size-of-place category.

4) Differences in voting behavior, along the general lines noted under points 1–3, prevailed in the special senatorial election of 1957 although the Democratic victory in that case was scored in unusual circumstances.

For the postwar period, at least, the voting data presented here undoubtedly illuminate the nature of Wisconsin's party system. The basis of the continued Republican victories through 1956 in state-wide elections and, as will be emphasized later, in the state legislature has been established. Republican majorities in medium-sized and especially in small cities and villages were sufficient to overcome Democratic majorities in large cities and to compensate for fluctuation in the farm vote. When the break came in 1957, the Republicans held only the small cities and villages which had been their strongest categories of strength, but their position in the medium-sized cities was not nearly so bad as in either the regularly Democratic large cities or the changeable farm townships.

No claim can be made for the universality of the Wisconsin findings with respect to the relation between size of place and the two-party division. Such work as has been done elsewhere on the general subject seldom relates specifically enough to the propositions analyzed here. However, certain studies have been cited which hold, more or less consistently with the first two findings, that there is a decrease in Democratic voting from larger to smaller cities. This is not to say that there is substantiation of the Wisconsin finding of one break between large and medium-sized places, and another between medium-sized and small places. Not only are detailed analyses in other states necessary to determine whether changes generally occur at these points, but such analyses would also be relevant to examining the question of whether a particularly strong Republicanism in smaller cities and villages is a function of a state's one-party background. Observation concerning the changeability of the farm vote coincides with general impressions of the political behavior of farmers in other states as well as in Wisconsin.[19] However, the degree of farm volatility relative to other segments of the electorate is not ordinarily discernible in analyses of election returns, particularly national returns. The farm vote is seldom separated from the much broader rural vote, and comparison is therefore difficult.

CHAPTER V

Party organizations

In their organization, contemporary Wisconsin parties exemplify a kind of political activism previously more familiar in Britain and continental Europe than in the United States. It is the largely nonpatronage organization of a regularized, often dues-paying, mass membership. The general absence of this type of organization in the United States has been emphasized, for example, in the best-known recent comparative study of parties,[1] and only a few exceptions other than in Wisconsin have been reported.[2] The ordinary American party appears to be skeletal, with its form prescribed by statute and its membership chiefly the few who themselves aspire to public office or public spoils.[3] Sustained recruitment of the larger number of committed partisans into permanent organizations useful for campaign activity remains fairly unusual in the United States.[4] The fact that it is exceptional is what makes the organization of Wisconsin parties especially interesting. However, the significance of the Wisconsin experience ought not be taken for granted. While, as will be shown, both party organizations seem to be permanent and growing, they could turn out to be limited to a place and a period instead of representing any general American political trend.

The special circumstances of the organizational development of Wisconsin parties have been described elsewhere,[5] and it is sufficient here to repeat that the parties being analyzed are the extralegal and voluntary agencies which perform virtually all consequential party functions. Attention is focussed on a relatively few features of party activism, particularly of local leadership, which could usefully be subject to comparative study in other states. In this way, it is hoped that the tentative findings about the nature of Wisconsin's new-model organizations will contribute on a small scale to the body of empirical knowledge essential to the eventual construction of a valid theory of political parties.

Although more than one method has been used, a large portion of the data derives from mail questionnaires sent early in 1957 to local party officers. Altogether 439 party officers received questionnaires, and these included Republican and Democratic chairmen and secretaries in almost all of the state's 71 counties, the chairman and a county council delegate from each of the active ward and suburban units of the Milwaukee County parties, and the presidents of women's Republican clubs (which admittedly are different from, though affiliated with, the regular party units). Of the 439 officers, 338 returned the questionnaires. The percentage returned was particularly high among officers of the regular county organizations. Only the Milwaukee ward and suburban officers show less than a three-quarters return, but here the original mailing was large enough so that most active units are represented in the tabulation. A copy of the questionnaire is in the Appendix.

Of at least equal importance is material gathered by interview and observation. In addition to detailed field studies of party activity in several counties, various state party personnel have been interviewed, and state conventions, as well as county and ward meetings, have been attended.

Specifically, in this chapter, certain hypotheses concerning the activism of voluntary nonpatronage parties are to be examined. These hypotheses are based partly on the demonstrated nature of such activism elsewhere, and partly on general impressions of the Wisconsin organizations. Broadly what is proposed is that the state's organized activism is a political phenomenon which can be distinguished from the customary American party by certain definite characteristics. In attempting to show these characteristics, one serious limitation of the present study is that many findings apply directly only to party officers, who are but one kind, and in some respects a distinct kind, of party activist. For this and for other reasons, only inconclusive answers can be given to the questions raised by the following hypotheses:

1) Large and highly organized memberships, where they exist, tend to coincide with urban and middle-class communities.[6]

2) Activists, as reflected by their leadership, are oriented mainly to national and state politics, rather than to local politics.

3) Party recruitment of officers reflects particular "political generations."

4) Republican leaders are drawn more heavily from high-status occupations than are Democratic leaders.

5) Competition for local party offices tends to be slight.

6) Party leadership is differentiated from candidacy for elective public office.

7) Party organizations, despite various limitations, tend to play an increasing part in the selection of candidates at least for state offices.

While these hypotheses, and the findings which follow, are stated in the present tense, it should be understood that they relate largely to party organizations as of 1956 and the years immediately preceding.

MEMBERSHIP

Two practical reasons might cause political leaders to try to enroll dues-paying party members. The first is to raise money directly from dues and related contributions, and the second is to obtain volunteer campaign services. These reasons are not pressing when party leaders or candidates have available, as is so often the case in the United States, large sums of money from a relatively few major contributors. Then there is no need for dues and little need for volunteers to do what can be bought through mass media of communications.

Wisconsin does not appear exceptional in these respects. Campaigns have been pretty well financed. Even in the off-year election of 1954, each party spent nearly one-quarter of a million dollars in campaigns for state and congressional offices.[7] Obviously money in this quantity had to be raised from sources other than members' dues. The major source of Republican funds has been a few hundred corporation executives, and the Democrats, at least until recently curbed by state law, collected substantial sums from unions.[8] Because of present restrictions on union contributions and because of limited access to wealthy individuals, the Democratic party has more financial cause than the Republicans to seek a broad membership base. However, the Republicans, even though well-financed in the past, have evidently found enough campaign use for members to enroll a following that is probably more numerous than that of the Democrats. Volunteer get-out-the-vote activity is considered a worthwhile supplement to large-scale advertising.

Before any details concerning membership are presented, the structure of the party organizations requires brief attention. Both Republicans and Democrats are based on county units generally, and also on ward and suburban level units in Milwaukee County. Federation takes place for certain limited purposes at the congressional level and more importantly at the state level. Each party holds an annual state convention, at which county units are represented, in the Republican case according to the number of votes cast in the county for the Republican gubernatorial candidate at the last election, and in the Democratic case mainly according to number of members in the county unit. State party headquarters are maintained on a year-round basis in Madison, and semiautonomous headquarters in Milwaukee County on the same basis. Regular headquarters staffs are small, ordinarily consisting of two people in each office, but they produce a steady stream of literature for the local units.

Ascertaining the number of party members is often difficult. For Wisconsin Democrats, however, the task is simplified by the existence of a state-wide dues-paying arrangement which, while the two-dollar dues are paid through county or ward units, gives the state headquarters an accurate count of unit memberships. Republican practice is more permissive; a growing number of county units have dues-paying memberships, but many others count as "members" those who make contributions, attend meetings, or simply appear on a mailing list. Common to both parties is a wide fluctuation, from year to year, in the membership of some units, although there is an upward trend in the state as a whole. The general order of magnitude is conveyed by the figure of 10,000 dues-paying state Democrats in 1956, and by the figures of 8,500 dues-paying Republicans in

Milwaukee County and of 1,000 in another smaller urban county in 1955.[9]

In the Republican case, the large dues-paying units are almost entirely urban county phenomena. Republican officers in several rural counties list between 100 and 300 members, but field inquiry in three such counties revealed that these organizations, while probably able to mobilize several hundred, did not in fact do so on any fixed basis. The organizations in these instances resemble the skeletal pattern usual enough in the United States, and they remain typical of much (though not all) of rural Republicanism in Wisconsin. As a former state Republican leader has said, a state-wide dues-paying arrangement would be resented by rural and traditional Republicans unaccustomed to having their affiliation formalized. On the positive side, the largest Milwaukee County Republican unit, and in fact the largest in the state, has over 2,300 dues payers in a suburban district with a total population of a fairly small county. The next largest Milwaukee Republican units are also in suburban districts or in upper-income city wards; organizations are small or almost nonexistent in working-class sections of the city. Elsewhere in the state, Republican units, including the women's clubs, tend to be relatively large in most counties having cities over 20,000, which provide sizable middle-class populations for party recruitment.

The dues-paying Democratic membership is also mainly but not entirely urban. Although Democratic-voting Milwaukee's total of 2,500 members is not large in relation to that county's population, most of the party's big and active units are in an urban environment. Only a few counties that are heavily farm or small-town in character have substantial organizations. The Democratic pattern also resembles the Republican in that membership often appears to be concentrated in middle-class residential areas. This is particularly striking in the state's second largest county, containing the capitol and the university, where there is a Democratic membership of over 1,000 located mostly in the Republican-voting side of the principal city rather than in Democratic-voting farm and working-class districts. Here as elsewhere there is an occasionally successful drive to sell memberships to union workers, but except for a few union leaders the year-to-year activists are mainly middle-class intellectuals. Consistent with this situation in a single county is the fact that state-wide Democratic membership does not generally coincide with Democratic voting strength. Thus the top 11 counties in their 1956 Democratic membership (expressed as a percentage of total votes in each county) ranked very differently on the basis of Democratic percentage of the 1956 gubernatorial vote; specifically, 2, 5, 13, 61, 36, 4, 45, 23, 26, 6, and 40.

Since an important object of large dues-paying organizations is to manage local get-out-the-vote campaigns, it is to the disadvantage of the Democrats to have their membership concentrated in middle-class areas rather than in the Democratic-oriented industrial sections, where, however, unions may effectively substitute for party in reaching the voters. Interestingly it is in some of Milwaukee's industrial wards that membership remains not only small and largely inactive, but patronage-oriented around the minor rewards of polling-booth jobs in a way untypical of the state. On the other hand, Republicans do seem most highly organized in their own voting strongholds, at least within urban communities. The large and active Republican membership in predominantly Republican suburbs and medium-sized cities is, of course, at odds with any notion that a *local* two-party competitive environment is necessary to stimulate organizational activity. On the contrary, it is the very sureness of the local Republican majorities that stimulates party leaders to build an organization capable of bringing out as many votes as possible to raise Republican totals in competitive state-wide and congressional elections.[10]

NATIONAL AND STATE ORIENTATIONS

The last observation indicates a membership oriented about national and state rather than local elections. The simplest way to check this point, it would seem, was to ask local party officers the elections and issues with which they were most concerned, but it turned out that many were reluctant to commit themselves (more so in mail questionnaires than in selected interviewing). When asked to choose an election they usually most wanted their party candidate to win, officers often checked all or most of the following items: president, governor, U.S. senator, U.S. representative, state legislator, and county courthouse officer. Similarly with respect to national, state, and county issues, more than one item was often checked. Systematic tabular presentation is therefore difficult. Of approximately 200 (of the 338 respondents) who did express an election preference, over half checked the presidential election, the next largest the governorship, and the fewest state legislative and courthouse positions. On issues, the indications of interest were similar, and these data, based on the 338 questionnaires,[11] may be simply presented:

> National issues 178
> State issues 129
> County issues 27
> Indefinite 73

There is no significant difference between competitive counties and heavily one-party counties, or between urban and rural counties. Also it is especially worth noting that Republican and Democratic preferences were about the same, contrary to the expectation that Republicans, entrenched in most Wisconsin courthouses, would be more concerned with county affairs than the Democrats. Evidently most local Republican party officers are set apart from career-oriented county courthouse occupants. Much of what interest party leaders did express in county elections appears, from interviews and marginal comments on questionnaires, to derive from an importance attached to having able local candidates as a means of strengthening state and national tickets.

Further information on the interests of party officers is provided in the tabulation of those attending party conventions (Table V-A). While the almost complete turnout shown for annual state conventions might have been assumed, the number attending national conventions is significantly high, especially for county chairmen and women's Republican club presidents, when it is appreciated how few delegates and alternates there can be from a state in any generation. It is fair to assume that the percentage of rank-and-file members attending national conventions would be much smaller than it is for county leaders, but this may not hold in the same degree for state conventions, which are highly social occasions especially for married couples. In stressing the national and state orientation of party activists, it is realized that a general concern with issues has been assumed, and that this assumption might seem to run counter to recent findings in the Detroit metropolitan area concerning the political preferences of those who consider themselves Republicans or Democrats. Specifically it was found there that regular party adherents were likely to perceive the differences between the two parties in various terms other than issues.[12] Nothing in the present study challenges this Detroit finding, but because data here are drawn only from actual party members, and mainly from party leaders, it is entirely possible that issues play a greater part than they did among the Detroit party adherents who were so classified by their voting regularity and self-identification as Republicans or Democrats.

The postwar Wisconsin parties, as American parties go, have had fairly consistent differences over state and national issues, and these differences look substantial enough so that they might account for policy commitments by party memberships. Even the state party platforms, though both follow the custom of making promises to all major economic groups, display some important differences of tone and content. Take the gubernatorial election year of 1954, for example, and especially the labor programs presented by each party. The Republicans, while reiterating their friendship for organized labor and their support of collective bargaining, declared their belief that the working man should have a right to a job without first joining a union and also the right to protection against unfair labor practices by union officials as well as employers. These items, though only mild manifestations of party misgivings about unions, found no place in the 100 per cent prolabor program of the Democrats. In addition to a substantial list of specific measures the Democrats promised to enact for labor's benefit, there was a pledge to repeal the state's "Labor Peace" Act which unions regarded as unfavorable in much the same way as the national Taft-Hartley law.

On state financial issues the difference between the two parties in 1954 was just as marked. While Republicans took pride in the reduction in income taxes made and maintained by their state administrations, Democrats advocated a whole list of new taxes affecting business and businessmen. The Democratic party would, for example, levy new taxes affecting railroads and banks, and restore the "privilege dividend" tax which Republicans had repealed some years before. And by promising relatively large, new expenditures in the fields of public welfare and education, in particular, the Democratic party indicated that it would, if in office, necessarily be a high-tax party. Thus, in a way that is familiar, the party of the left displayed its concern to extend the boundaries of the welfare state. And conversely Wisconsin Republicans were typical of contemporary right-wing parties. They were willing enough to preserve the welfare programs which existed, and even extend them here and there, but the countervalues of economy and low taxes were important determinants of the party's general position.

Economy and taxes were also determinants in fixing Wisconsin Republican positions on national issues, particularly those concerning foreign policy, which were in the forefront of public discussion during the postwar years. Here party lines between the state's Republicans and Democrats have sharply diverged. While Democrats were fully committed to the defense of the foreign policy of the Truman Administration, Republicans in Wisconsin were among the most vigorous and best-known critics of that policy. Their criticism became especially prominent after Senator Joseph McCarthy launched his attack on the State Department in 1950. Wisconsin Republicans found McCarthy's campaign very much to their taste, and for a few years he was the most popular figure at party gatherings. The few Republican leaders who might have been lukewarm about McCarthy found it expedient to refrain from dissent. Thus party differences over foreign policy, setting off Republicans from Democrats, also became party differences over the controversial senator.

More lasting than their McCarthyite support, however, has been the general anti-internationalism of Wisconsin Republicans. It is this which survived the decline and death of Senator McCarthy. The residual isolationism represented by Senator

Taft has been the compelling ideological commitment. Thus the state organization has remained notably unenthusiastic about the foreign policy of the Eisenhower Administration and also of the senior Republican senator from Wisconsin, Alexander Wiley. As late as June, 1955, the Wisconsin Republican convention singled out McCarthy for its praise, refused to commend Wiley by name, and commended President Eisenhower only after a prolonged battle.[13] This same convention, like its predecessors of recent years, went on record in favor of the essence of the proposed Bricker Amendment to restrict the President's treaty-making powers. Again in 1956 the Bricker proposal was endorsed,[14] and in 1957 the Republican convention turned its fire against the NATO status-of-forces treaties.[15] These sentiments, among many others it is true, found expression in the decision of the 1956 Republican convention to endorse a congressional critic of internationalism against the primary candidacy of Senator Wiley. This decision, as well as the regular anti-internationalist resolutions, undoubtedly reflected views held steadfastly and enthusiastically by almost all of the two to three thousand delegates.

Just as completely, the members of the Democratic party of Wisconsin have assumed northern liberal positions on national issues, concerning domestic as well as foreign affairs. The New Deal–Fair Deal ideology has been faithfully adopted with respect to labor, social security, farm parity, and civil rights. The liberal antagonism to McCarthyism was especially prominent as a focal point for middle-class intellectuals in the early 1950's.

POLITICAL GENERATIONS

The concept of political generations might be especially fruitful in an analysis of party activists whose motivation is strongly suspected to relate to issues. If it could be shown that substantial numbers joined because of particular issues at particular times (i.e., New Deal Democrats, McCarthyites, or Eisenhower Republicans), not only would there be strong support for the issue-motivation theory but also there would be a great deal more knowledge about the general nature of parties. No such definite findings can be reported here, and indeed it would

seem difficult to do so without systematic interviewing of a carefully selected sample of party activists. The limited data of the
mail questionnaires (Table 6) are only suggestive.

Table 6

MEDIAN YEARS OF WISCONSIN PARTY MEMBERSHIP
AND OF ACTIVE PARTY WORK

Party Officers	Party Members		Party Workers	
	N	Median yrs.	N	Median yrs.
Republicans				
County chairmen	62	21	62	16.5
County secretaries	54	12	58	10
Women's club presidents	39	20	38	8
Milwaukee unit officers	22	10.5	22	10
Democrats				
County chairmen	62	10	62	7
County secretaries	63	10	63	6
Milwaukee unit officers	26	8	26	7

It may be seen from Table 6 that the median years of both
party membership and party activity are markedly higher for
Republicans than for Democrats, particularly among county
chairmen. Since membership is an elusive conception when and
where dues-paying has not been instituted, the number of years
as an active party worker provides a more reliable basis for
comparison. Closer analysis of the answers to this item reveals
an interesting bimodal distribution of Republican county chairmen, about one-quarter of whom have been active six to ten
years and another quarter sixteen to twenty years. On the other
hand, about two-thirds of the Democratic county chairmen fall
in the two lowest brackets (that is, one to ten years). Thus
Republican leadership, while of older party service on the average than the Democratic, is not uniformly so since much of its
recruitment has also been in the postwar decade—the decade,
that is, of both McCarthy and Eisenhower. Among the Democrats, the low median and the low mode are clear reflections of
the party's postwar character as an active organization in Wisconsin, and thus of the generation of New Dealers, Fair Dealers,
and ex-Progressives who entered that organization.[16]

Observation of state conventions, previously noted, has some
bearing on the political generations represented. The demon-

strated anti-internationalism of Republican activists during the
1950's might represent the pre-1940 generation of activists
(that is, the sixteen- to twenty-year men) or a more recently
recruited neoisolationist generation, or both these generations.
It is evident that an Eisenhower generation was not dominant.
Such a generation, if recruited, especially in the suburbs, since
1952, was not yet heavily represented at party leadership levels
(although it has been represented by some Republican officeholders). The Democratic party is less complicated in this respect, since the nearly universal acceptance of the New Deal–
Fair Deal ideology is fully consistent with the dominance of the
Roosevelt-Truman generation of activists at party conventions.

OCCUPATIONAL STATUS

Data on occupations of party officers are shown in detail in
Table V-B. The preponderance of professional and business-
managerial classes is especially apparent when the housewife
category is temporarily ignored. The percentages of manual
workers, sales-clerical personnel, and farmers are generally low,
and particularly low when Republican officers are considered
alone. Applying these generalizations about party officers to all
party activists is obviously risky. However, observation of several county and ward units leads one to believe that the officers
are representative of their memberships in terms of broad occupational status. The previously described location of the larger
memberships in middle-class urban neighborhoods is also
relevant.

Along with the housewife category, women officers in general deserve some special comment because they are so numerous not only in the case of women's Republican clubs but also
among secretaries of both parties, particularly of the Democrats.
In the latter instance, thirty-one of the sixty-five secretaries are
women, fewer than half of whom are housewives. In both
parties, women tend to be unit secretaries more frequently in
urban than in rural counties. Nevertheless, even where numerous, the number of women holding party office probably under-
states the degree of activism by women. Male chairmen interviewed in selected counties have readily granted that women—
especially wives of business and professional men—do most of

the party's get-out-the-vote work. In this respect the Republican women, though in their own club, act much as the Democratic women do within the regular county organization.

The larger percentage of high-status occupations among Republican than among Democratic officers is an obvious feature of Table V-B. Notably in the case of county chairmen, over twice as many Republicans are business or professional men. The difference between Republican and Democratic unit officers in Milwaukee is not so sharp, no doubt because there are many wards in which business and professional residents are scarce for both parties. Still here, as elsewhere in urban areas, there is a higher Democratic percentage of manual workers, just as there are more farmers among Democratic officers in rural areas. Incidentally it should be noted that the fairly numerous local government officials among Republican secretaries are found mainly in rural counties where the party organization is not large or highly developed. However, with respect to the generalization that Republican officers are drawn more heavily than Democrats from business and professional classes, there is no substantial difference between urban and rural counties, or between competitive and one-party Republican counties.[17]

While this general difference between Republican and Democratic officers is large enough to be significant, it is not nearly so marked as the occupational difference that has elsewhere been shown to exist between Republican and Democratic voting adherents.[18] It may thus be more important to note that many Democratic officers are business and professional men, rather than to emphasize how few they are relative to the number among Republican officers. Further reason for this emphasis is found in the observation that the larger and more active Democratic units seem, like the Republican, to have a leadership as well as a membership drawn from higher-status occupations. The weaker units, on the other hand, are thought by state Democratic officials to be weak partly because they lack such leadership. This is applied to working-class units in Milwaukee (where, however, union personnel occasionally supply some intellectual leadership) and particularly to units in one-party Republican counties, where there is hardly any business or professional talent available to the Democrats.[19]

COMPETITION FOR LOCAL PARTY
OFFICES

In these nonpatronage organizations which seem so far to be largely service units for state and national candidates, local party offices might be regarded as unwelcome burdens. In that case, contests for such offices should be decidedly exceptional, and the duties of chairman and secretary annually passed around from one reluctant volunteer to another. Situations of this sort have been observed, but that they are usual is less than half-supported by answers from county unit heads to the question, "In 1956 or 1957 has there been a contest for any office in your local party organization?" Contests were reported in 39 per cent of the Republican county organizations, 46 per cent of the women's Republican clubs, and 59 per cent of the Democratic county organizations.[20] No significantly different pattern emerged in urban as distinct from rural counties, or in competitive as opposed to one-party counties. The fairly frequent contests might conceivably result from long-range ambitions for political careers, from factionalism, or simply from the desire of the volunteer activist to gain the additional psychic income that goes with party leadership in the cause to which he is devoted. Local officers do receive some public recognition; for example, in 1957 the new Republican governor entertained his party's county chairmen at a reception at the executive mansion.

ROLES OF LEADERS AND CANDIDATES

Although many potential candidates for public office, it may be observed, do become members and more or less active in the organizational cause, it is clear that they could not very well constitute any large proportion of a mass-membership party. The essence of such a party is that it contains activists who, because of choice or circumstances, are unlikely to run for public office. While this is the impression conveyed by Wisconsin party activists as a group, the party officer questionnaires do not offer convincing evidence on this point for the leadership. Admittedly, however, it would be surprising if officers were not more likely election candidates than rank-and-file activists.

Table V-C shows that the roles of party leaders and candidates for public office were by no means mutually exclusive, whether measured by actual elections, defeats, or future plans. This is still more apparent from another calculation that shows that only about half the officers said they had been *neither* elected to nor defeated for public office (whereas about two-thirds, as shown in Table V-C, said *no* to each question separately). Even this group of roughly 50 per cent of the party officers cannot be described as a hard core of noncandidates since some may want to run in the future. Nor can the "do-not-intends" or "do-not-desires" of Table V-C be taken as definite noncandidates because some may have run in the past. The hard core is best approximated by counting how many of the negatively intending or the negatively desiring had never been candidates in the past. The results show that 43.5 per cent of all 338 officers neither *intended* to run nor had run in the past, and that 34.6 per cent neither *desired* to run nor had run before. Either percentage represents a fairly substantial group of noncandidates, but fewer county chairmen and more women's club presidents than other officers are in the group.

Closer analysis of the questionnaires indicates the need for some qualification of the percentages reported above. Although no sharp rural-urban difference is discernible, there is a difference between one-party and competitive situations. Thus the Democrats, more of whom were defeated candidates, tended to be sacrificial rather than serious nominees in one-party Republican counties. By filling their party's state legislative or courthouse ticket, and so making the ballot look better for national and state candidates, Democratic leaders were still in their role as activists rather than as aspiring officeholders. For example, of 35 Democratic county chairmen defeated for public office, 20 lost in the 36 counties tabulated as safe-Republican. The same explanation, in reverse, helps to account for the large number of Republican ward officers defeated for public office in Democratic Milwaukee County. Interviews have generally confirmed this explanation.

Another kind of qualification is indicated by questionnaire information on the names of offices elected-to or defeated-for. Particularly among Republican county chairmen, whose percentage elected to office was the highest of any group's, it is noteworthy that of 46 public offices held (by 33 chairmen) 31 were nonpartisan elective offices, many of them virtually unremunerative. The pattern is roughly similar for other party officers.

Despite these several qualifications, however, it is still impossible to be sure that many more than one-third to one-half of the party leaders have ruled out the role of candidates for remunerative public office. However, even this conservatively estimated proportion seems high when compared with the leadership of an old-style organization like that of Chicago's ward committeemen, very few of whom, Gosnell found, held no governmental position.[21]

CANDIDATE SELECTION

There remains the question of the part played by party leaders and their organizations in selecting candidates for public office. Put differently, this is to ask whether Wisconsin's organized activists exercise power over nominations, or whether they merely help elect party nominees. For any kind of formal control over nominations, it ought to be mentioned again that the state provides a most uncongenial environment. The open primary and the political customs accompanying it operate against effective organizational influence. However, such influence is not entirely prevented by law or custom, and the evidence of party efforts to exert influence in the nominating process deserves close examination. The evidence is apparent in the Republican case in a way that it cannot be in the Democratic. By its own constitutional provision, the Democratic party prohibits its units at all levels from officially endorsing candidates in primary elections. No such prohibition is maintained by the Republicans; on the contrary, the Republican party constitution requires the state convention to give pre-primary endorsement to a candidate for each state-wide office in regular election years. In addition, Republican endorsement is customary at the congressional level.

For county and state legislative offices, there is much less difference between Republican and Democratic practices. Even though allowed to endorse, Republican county or ward units rarely do so. The absence in both parties of local-level endorsement is consistent with the apparently lesser interest of party activists in local as opposed to state and national elections. But this lesser interest falls short of accounting for failure to endorse state legislative candidates, who, while locally elected, are chosen to deal with state issues. In fact, party officers do seem interested in state legislative business; almost all of those who were represented by a legislator of their own party reported on their questionnaires that they took the opportunity to discuss legislative business with their senator or assemblyman. Furthermore, with respect to legislative candidacies, over 86 per cent of the party officers said that in 1956 they did one or more of the following: encouraged well-qualified candidates, sought well-qualified candidates, persuaded such candidates, or tried to dissuade individuals from entering the primary against a well-qualified candidate already in the race. While these results indicate party interest, to be sure, they do not mean that much influence is claimed. Only 34 of 338 officers asserted even as much attempted control as is implied by trying to dissuade individuals. The popular choices, in order of frequency, were encouraging, seeking, and persuading candidates, and these answers are compatible with the not-very-influential activity of filling the party ticket in hopeless races. This particular subject, however, is to be examined from another angle in Chapter Seven on legislative elections, and it is only necessary to add here that the data obtained from legislators, as well as from field studies, tend to confirm the general impression of limited organizational influence at this level.

Here it is useful to return to the state level and observe in Republican endorsement procedure an excellent example of a political organization seeking to play what Key has called "a positive role in leadership." [22] Gathering two or three thousand activists as delegates in May or June of each regular election year, the Republican state convention has since 1950, when endorsement became mandatory, endorsed single candidates in the September primary for governor, other state constitutional offices, and U.S. senator. This enables the full force of party finance and activity to affect the primary campaign. Before 1950, this endorsement procedure had been employed occasionally, but the failure to do so in 1948, when at least two winning Republican primary candidates were regarded as unsuitable within the organization, convinced party leaders that they needed to make future endorsement mandatory, as they did in 1949, and thus prevent a particular convention from avoiding a difficult choice among candidates. This suggests that endorsement has not been universally popular among Republicans, and so it seemed as late as 1957 when, meeting in their off-year convention, the party refused to endorse any of six candidates in the special primary election to choose a Republican nominee for the late Senator McCarthy's seat.[23] (This refusal was technically consistent with the party's constitution which required endorsements only at conventions meeting in even-numbered years—that is, in the regular election years.)

In the years from 1950 through 1956, the Republican endorsement procedure appears fairly, but not entirely, successful in controlling the party nomination. At all four elections, the endorsed candidate for governor won the primary (twice as an incumbent), and only once was he even opposed. For the four lesser state constitutional offices, endorsed candidates won each time except for secretary of state. Here on two occasions the organization failed to defeat the long-time incumbent, Fred Zimmerman, a maverick Republican of great popularity, and on a third occasion, after Zimmerman's death, failed to defeat his son. These failures were hardly signs of organizational weakness. On the contrary, mounting a substantial opposition to the Zimmerman reputation indicated confidence and strength. Even more impressive, of course, was the actual success of the Republican organization in 1954 when its endorsed choice for lieutenant governor did win the primary over a three-term incumbent with the politically redoubtable name of George Smith.[24]

More often raised to question the effectiveness of Republican endorsement is the primary contest for U.S. senator in 1956. It was then that the party convention endorsed Congressman Glenn Davis against the internationalist Alexander Wiley, the three-term incumbent and the ranking minority member of the

Senate foreign relations committee.[25] Davis did lose, but it is really a tribute to the organization that, in his first state-wide race, Davis ran less than 10,000 votes behind an established incumbent in a total Republican primary poll of about 450,000. Without Wisconsin's familiar crossover of Democratic voters to the Republican primary, encouraged especially in this instance by the usually pro-Democratic *Milwaukee Journal*'s support of Wiley, it may fairly be assumed that Davis would have won. It is understandable that subsequently Republican party leaders should have sought, though unsuccessfully in 1957, to persuade their convention to go on record in favor of a closed rather than an open primary.[26] No doubt such a change would enhance the value of endorsement, but even under the present law Republican organizational support has proved to be sufficient except in the particularly difficult cases.

In light of the Republican experience, several Democratic party leaders have become interested in the endorsement procedure and have begun, in some instances, to advocate that their party adopt it. In 1957, the Democratic administrative committee formally proposed endorsement, but the party convention of that fall, at the urging of its just-elected U.S. Senator, William Proxmire, boisterously rejected the proposal.[27] Although a future change was not thus precluded, it is fair to say that endorsement remains highly unpopular with most Democratic activists. Opposition to endorsement stems from the Democratic inheritance of the old progressive antimachine tradition associated with the first La Follette's successful substitution of the direct primary for the "boss-ridden" Republican convention. For old La Follette supporters, anything that resembles convention control over nominations is antidemocratic, and it is too much for the organization even to seek to direct the voter's choice in the primary.[28] Democratic leaders proposing endorsement have readily been criticized as emulators of the Republican tactics which anticonservative forces in Wisconsin have long opposed.[29]

This antiorganizational spirit, discussed in Chapter Two as part of the Wisconsin background, cannot readily be dismissed. Not only has it been invoked to prevent Democratic endorsement altogether, but it has been played to with apparent effectiveness in Republican primaries by candidates who, like Senator Wiley, fought against candidates endorsed by the party. Conceivably this spirit might diminish if Wisconsin's new-model parties were to grow in size and respectability, thus becoming more distinct, in the public mind, from old-fashioned political machines. On the basis of that kind of development, one might more confidently predict greater and more effective organizational activity in the selection of candidates generally.

SUMMARY

Tentative findings related to the original hypotheses about Wisconsin's party activism may be briefly summarized:

1) Generally, large and highly organized memberships are found in urban and suburban middle-class communities.

2) Orientation mainly to national and state politics is indicated by party officers, and this seems related to the fact that local units tend to be large and active regardless of the absence of competition in local elections. Policy differences between the state's parties have been fairly sharp.

3) Data from local party officers suggest the dominance of Democratic leadership by a New Deal–Fair Deal generation recruited in the postwar years, and the presence of two separate generations of Republicans, prewar and postwar.

4) Although local Republican leadership is more homogeneous occupationally than that of the Democrats, it may be more significant that the leadership of both parties is drawn heavily from high-status occupations.

5) Considerable competition for local party offices, contrary to subjective impressions, is reported by leaders.

6) Roles of party leaders and candidates for public office are often not mutually exclusive. Nevertheless a substantial number of local officers do seem unlikely to be serious candidates for remunerative political offices.

7) In contrast apparently to the situation at the local level, there is at least for state-wide offices a significant degree of Republican organizational activity in selecting candidates, and some tendency for similar Democratic activity to develop.

This last point is especially interesting in light of the other findings. If, as postulated and to some extent demonstrated, the

Wisconsin mass-membership parties have characteristics distinguishing them from traditional American parties, then it becomes important to know the extent to which these agencies are to become determinants of candidacies, and so perhaps of policies. That they will be completely decisive determinants seems unlikely. In Wisconsin as in most of the United States, thanks to the primary, activists cannot bestow the party label with the finality of, say, a British constituency association. The inability to do this may seriously limit the function of mass parties in the United States. Nevertheless the Wisconsin experience to date indicates that fairly large voluntary organizations can at least exist without complete control of the nominating process, and sometimes without even trying to control it.

CHAPTER VI

Legislative membership and political careers

IN this and the following chapter, the Wisconsin legislature provides the material for the analysis of selected elements in the recruitment of political personnel. Rather than being concerned, as in the preceding chapter, with those who are primarily party activists, attention is now focussed on political personnel in the category of officeholders and aspiring officeholders. For this purpose, the state legislature is most convenient. Its membership of 133 is large enough to include a significant number of Wisconsin politicians at any given time, and because of the biennial election of all 100 assemblymen and either 16 or 17 of the 33 senators, there are sufficient contests in each election year to permit generalization. Also legislators are located in the hierarchy of political positions at a beginning level of policymaking and issue-orientation. In this respect, state legislative positions are more nearly in the political channel of higher state and national offices than are county or nonpartisan municipal positions.

Reserving the subject of legislative elections to the next chapter, the discussion here is limited to the characteristics of the state legislative positions and especially of the politicians who hold these positions, and to the place of such positions in political careers. On these topics, there are certain propositions, emerging from general knowledge of state legislators and to some extent from other studies, which are to be critically examined in light of Wisconsin data. These propositions, or hypotheses, are as follows:

1) Status and salary of state legislators are not so high as to prevent a heavy voluntary withdrawal.

70116

2) Rural legislators have deeper local roots, less formal education, and more political experience, and are older and less likely to have professional or business-managerial occupations than urban legislators.

3) Legislators are an upwardly mobile group occupationally, and this is especially true for lawyers.

4) Legislative positions serve in significant degree as steps in individual careers.

While some of these propositions are subjected to tests based on historical data, the bulk of the material in this chapter (and the following chapter) relates to the 1957 legislature. When available, as it is on some matters from official compilations, information on all 133 legislators is tabulated. However, on many topics data were gathered from interviews and mail questionnaires, and only 111 of the 133 legislators responded with information as requested. Although 111 represent a high proportion of the total, nevertheless it may be thought that the missing 22 legislators have something in common that is not accurately reflected by the 111 respondents. This possibility cannot be dismissed, but it seems remote after comparing the 111 respondents with the full membership of 133 for those items on which official information is available. As shown in Table VI-A, the 111 represent the full legislature fairly closely with respect to age, education, party, urban-rural status, occupation, Senate as opposed to Assembly membership, length of service, and nature of party competition in respective districts. The exception is in occupations, where the sales-clerical and retired categories are understated.

This is the place to define a set of terms used in this chapter and the next. *Urban* and *rural,* when referring to legislative districts, are given a special meaning different from the U.S. Census use of the same terms. An urban district is any in which over half the population live in a city or cities over 10,000, or in a Census-classified urbanized area. All other districts are called rural, and so include those in which over half of the population live in cities and villages below 10,000, on farms, or in a combination of the two. Although this means calling *rural* many places above 2,500, where the Census line is drawn, it is believed that the level of 10,000 population represents a more realistic political dividing line, as indicated by the analysis, in Chapter Four, of size of place in relation to the two-party vote. Incidentally of the 61 urban legislators, 32 are from Milwaukee County.

STATUS AND TURNOVER

Legislative service in Wisconsin as elsewhere is not a full-time occupation. Unlike U.S. congressmen, state legislators are not in session or otherwise engaged in official business so much of the time that they are unable to maintain their private occupations. Nor are state legislators generally paid enough so that they can afford to abandon their private economic pursuits. Yet legislators at least in Wisconsin and other larger states are also some distance removed from a situation in which their governmental duties could be regarded as so slight as to affect hardly at all their outside income-earning capacity. The fact is that state legislative service is in between the full-time congressional or administrative positions and the obviously part-time functions of most local aldermen or school board members. In larger urban states, legislators are nearer to the congressional type; and in rural states, to the poorly paid volunteer.[1] While state legislative service is not generally professionalized as a full-time career in the way so typical of Congress, it may be moving in that direction as governmental affairs become more numerous and more complex.[2]

The Wisconsin legislature does not meet annually in the manner of legislatures in many large states, but only in odd-numbered years. Sessions start in January and usually run through much of June, plus a few weeks in the fall of the same year. Seven months are about the outside limit of actual legislative session, but many legislators now serve on the Legislative Council's study committees which meet from time to time between sessions. Work on these committees is increasing and tending to make some degree of legislative service more nearly a year-round affair. However, even during the seven months of actual session, service is a little short of full-time. In the first few months of each session, legislative work is ordinarily confined to Tuesday, Wednesday, and Thursday of each week so that members have a few days for their own business at home.

Of course, the shorter the distance from a legislator's home to the state capitol, the greater the opportunity for him to transact his local business. Metropolitan representatives from Milwaukee, it ought to be noted, are eighty miles from home when they are at the state capitol in Madison and therefore only fairly well situated for business purposes. Legislators from Madison itself have an obvious advantage. Most other urban representatives, and also many rural legislators, live farther from the capitol than do the Milwaukeeans.

Establishing compensation suitable to this quasi-part-time employment is awkward. Through the 1957 session, Wisconsin paid its legislators, apart from travel expenses, $200 a month (that is, $4,800 for the biennium) plus $100 a month room-and-board allowance when the legislature was in session. This amounted to more than the figure in most states, but it was less than the amount paid by eight more populous states, and particularly below the biennial salaries of $15,000 in New York, $12,000 in California, and $10,000 in New Jersey, Ohio, and Illinois.[3] All but the last two states held annual sessions, which were contemplated but not adopted by Wisconsin in 1957. Nevertheless increased future payments were approved in 1957. The new scale raises the basic legislative salary to $300 (from $200) and the sessional room-and-board allowance to $175 (from $100). Thus apart from travel the total biennial payment of salary and expense allowances, assuming seven months of legislative session, is to be $8,425 compared to $5,500 under the old scale.

The new level represents a substantial increase, to be sure, but since many legislators spend at least as much living temporarily in the capital city as they are paid in expense allowances, the net income is still unimpressive as an alternative to urban business and professional possibilities. True enough, an unconscientious legislator, performing few if any duties between sessions, would have been able to retain some of his salary or allowances if he roomed at the Madison Y.M.C.A. during sessions and regularly ate and drank as the guest of lobbyists (a custom entirely legal until the special fall session of the 1957 legislature sought to prohibit it). However, it is improbable that the legislative salary and allowances would be attractive for many able business or professional men accustomed to living well on their own resources. Their incentive to be legislators must involve something other than salary, even at the new figure. Taking at least seven months off every biennium from one's regular occupation, especially if it is growing in remuneration, is likely, except for the most fortunately situated, to be more costly in the long run than can be compensated for by the new salary. Thus it is reasonable to assume that Wisconsin's increased payments will not greatly change the general status of legislative positions. In and of themselves, these positions are not sufficiently remunerative to substitute for full-time occupations of prosperous individuals.

Generally the financial disadvantages of state legislative service are greater in higher-cost and higher-income urban areas than in rural areas. A special aspect of this arises in comparing the legislative pay scale to that for other elective positions in Wisconsin. Thus a state legislator's pay compares favorably to that of a rural district attorney, but not to that of a district attorney in a metropolitan county. Even more telling is the fact that state legislators receive much less than do members of the Milwaukee County board and members of the Milwaukee city council, who are paid over $14,000 biennially in each case. It is no wonder that Milwaukee's state legislators often seek promotion by election to their county or city agencies. There is another and less tangible difference in status between metropolitan legislators, or perhaps urban legislators generally, and rural legislators. The latter seem more important and prestigious in their communities than do legislators who come from cities, particularly large cities. Perhaps this reflects the absence in rural areas of any well-publicized unit of government, like that of a large municipality, competing for importance and attention with the state government. At any rate, there is a general impression that the rural legislator is locally better known and of higher status in his district than is the representative from a big city.

In the capital itself, legislators have a rather special status. During sessions they may become minor public figures mentioned regularly in newspaper stories, and because of their powers they receive flattering attention from interest groups, ranging from the state university to the tavern-keepers' association. This attention has often taken the form of dinner-table and barroom camaraderie, stimulated by the generosity of lobbyists, and this social life has provided compensation for the legislator's forced abandonment of home life during the weekdays of legislative sessions. Incidentally the provision of food and drink by lobbyists has appeared to be a somewhat larger part of interest-group activity in the state capital than it has in the more sophisticated atmosphere of Washington.

However, free meals and drinks must be regarded as only minor pecuniary advantages, which may now be effectively prohibited. More substantial financial opportunities might be available, in or out of session, to an influential legislator who, if he were a lawyer, could represent clients before state boards and commissions. One such opportunity was curtailed in 1957, following a scandal, by the governor's order that legislators could no longer represent clients in pardon hearings,[4] but there is no such prohibition with respect to other matters. Yet it is by no means clear that there is necessarily a net profit to be made from appearances before state boards and commissions, since clients often expect a lawyer-legislator from their own district to argue their cases without fee and as part of their representative function. Altogether it seems hard to establish that a legislator can use his office to obtain a large additional income unless he is corrupt in the obvious and legal sense of that term. This is not to deny that a legislator's service may contribute to his future career and income-earning potential, as well as to his present psychic income and social pleasure. It is only to contend that actually being a legislator is not itself highly remunerative, if indeed it is remunerative at all.

This view is related to the high turnover in legislative personnel. That there is such a turnover is apparent from the evidence, shown in Table VI-B, that fewer than half the 1957 legislators have served more than two terms and fewer than 30 per cent more than three terms. In this respect, Wisconsin's recent experience appears to be consistent with what is known of legislatures elsewhere. The pattern was the same twenty years ago when Charles S. Hyneman studied legislative turnover in ten states.[5] In his thorough study, Hyneman also found that election defeats accounted for only a small proportion of the turnover. Similarly in Wisconsin, as shown in connection with the discussion in the next chapter, in the six elections between 1946 and 1956, fewer than half of those not re-elected had actually sought re-election. The remainder, as in Hyneman's ten states, are assumed to represent voluntary withdrawals except in instances of death or serious ill-health. Nothing in the impression of Wisconsin's recent experience, as confirmed by conversation with legislators, would cause one to dissent from Hyneman's opinion that "the chief reason why legislators find one or two terms enough is a financial one; their experience proves what they already suspected—that it is money out of the pocket to serve in the legislature." [6] This statement should be understood as meaning not that it is "money out of the pocket" for *all* legislators, but that it is so, especially in terms of outside business and professional loss, for those legislators who withdraw, or at least for many of them.

Further detail on legislative turnover, though not on its causes, is presented in Table VI-B. The breakdown there between Senate and Assembly indicates more seniority among senators, particularly since their terms are four years rather than two. Also the fact that many senators have previously served in the Assembly is an important contribution to their total legislative experience. Nevertheless the concentration of senators, like assemblymen, in the categories of only one or two terms is impressive. One qualification should be made. The even higher-than-usual number of first-term assemblymen in 1955 and of first-term senators in 1955 and 1957 probably reflects the substitution of new urban districts for old rural ones as a result of the reapportionment which took effect in 1954 and in 1956 (for 16 Senate seats). However, in none of the years, 1951–1957, on which the table is based, was there a sharp party overturn.

Whether the relatively brief service that has been characteristic of Wisconsin legislators is in the public interest remains to be noted. Hyneman, attaching considerable value to the usefulness of experience in the legislative process, thought that the high turnover was decidedly bad. On the other side, there is an argument in favor of periodic renewal on the ground that it is more democratic than having a corps of professional representatives. This democratic argument, it is plain from the facts concerning the large number of voluntary withdrawals, must be made without depending on the virtues of a new man defeating an incumbent in an election based on the incumbent's record. Nevertheless it is an argument entirely compatible with the traditional American conception of legislation by representatives who are primarily citizens and only incidentally office-holding politicians. Neither the increases in work nor in pay have so far, in Wisconsin at any rate, entirely destroyed this conception. The state legislature has edged a little closer to professionalization, but it is still some distance from being a full-time occupation of long-run attractiveness to the bulk of its membership. In this respect, Wisconsin may be at a transitional stage, perhaps intermediate between the smaller, more rural states and the larger, more urban states. It would be useful to have comparative studies of postwar legislative turnover in several states.

SOCIOECONOMIC CHARACTERISTICS

In examining the socioeconomic characteristics of legislators, particularly in the 1957 session, emphasis is to be placed on a comparison of what is hypothesized as differing urban and rural political styles. However, the characteristics of legislators in general are also noteworthy. One is the great predominance of males. In the 1957 session there were no women, and in the previous two sessions there was but one. The high point in postwar years was two women in 1949 and 1951. Since this pattern resembles American experience generally, the absence of women in the Wisconsin legislature may be explained in large part by their usually assumed reluctance actively to seek partisan office. Also there is an atmosphere of the male club about a legislative body which is discouraging and difficult for women to appreciate (and to be appreciated in). Economically, however, legislative service might be better suited to the situation of many women, for example, middle-class wives without young children, than to their husbands. In such a leisure class, there is undoubtedly a large reservoir of educated female ability available for, but not drawn into, legislative service. It is striking that election to public office at this level is seldom taken as an alternative to activity in the League of Women Voters or in local party organizations. In particular, the absence of women in the legislature contrasts sharply with their very active role in local parties, as discussed in Chapter Five.

Age

The median age for all members of the 1957 legislature is 49, but, as shown in Table VI-C, the concentration of legislators about this median is not especially heavy. Rather the age distribution is such that there are nearly equal numbers of members in each of the five categories: under 35, 36 to 45, 46 to 55, 56 to 65, and 66 and over. There is no "typical" age bracket.[7]

Separate analysis of those 45 and under, that is the two youngest categories of Table VI-C, reveals some significant facts. Among Democratic legislators, those 45 years old or less constitute 48.8 per cent, compared to 35.6 per cent of the Republicans. There is a similar difference between urban and rural legislators, which is not surprising in light of the relation of urbanism to Democratic representation. Among urban legislators, 49.2 per cent are no more than age 45, compared to 31.9 per cent of rural legislators. This urban-rural difference, it will be noted, is slightly greater than that between Democrats and Republicans, and Table VI-C shows that the proportion 45 or less is higher among urban than among rural Republicans.

Besides the Democratic and even more decidedly urban preponderance within the younger group of legislators, there is another quality that is even more striking. Of the 53 legislators who are 45 or less, 33 are lawyers although there are altogether only 40 lawyers in the legislature. Put differently, 82.5 per cent of the lawyers and only 21.5 per cent of the nonlawyers in the legislature are age 45 or less. The relative youthfulness of lawyer-legislators is pertinent to the special discussion of lawyers near the end of this chapter.

Local roots

Although American customs with respect to local residence of legislative representatives, in contrast to British practice for instance, are such as to attach political value generally to lifelong or near lifelong community attachments, it would seem likely that this value would be less pervasive in growing and changing urban areas than in rural communities. However, this particular hypothesis is not supported by data obtained from 1957 legislators. As may be noted in Table VI-D, hardly any difference exists between the percentages of urban and of rural legislators who have lived in their respective counties more than thirty years. In each case, the figure is at least 70 per cent, indicating that the great majority of all legislators have maintained long local residence and that at least most younger legislators, more of whom are urban, have lived virtually all of their lives in the counties from which they have been elected.

The urban-rural similarity ends when years of district residence are compared, as in the lower half of Table VI-D. Urban legislators record significantly fewer years in their respective districts than do rural legislators. Obviously this reflects the mobility of residents within large urban counties as well as the recent reapportionment that created new metropolitan districts. It indicates that an urban legislator has a different kind of local attachment, but not therefore a lesser one, than the rural legislator. He is just as likely to have a long residence in a given county, but because of the nature of his urban county (particularly metropolitan Milwaukee County) he is less likely to have a long residence in his district. Under the law, a legislator must reside in his district at the time of his election, but he may move to the district just when he decides to run. Although one such extreme case of intracounty mobility has been observed, it cannot occur often in view of the low percentage of urban legislators living less than ten years in their districts. Indeed the political meaning of the urban-rural difference in district residence seems limited in import as long as the demonstrated similarity exists in length of county residence. Urban legislators are almost as local as they can be in view of the necessarily arbitrary and shifting district lines in large cities.

Political experience

In Wisconsin, rural legislators are widely believed to have more political experience than urban legislators. Partly this belief may rest on the greater age of rural legislators, as already shown, but age alone is hardly a sufficient standard. Political experience is more usually measured by length of service in one's present office and by other offices held. On the first score, as tabulated in Table VI-E, the data for assemblymen alone should be emphasized since the senators are too few in each category for the percentages to be meaningful. Rural assemblymen may be seen to have served somewhat longer than urban assemblymen, but the difference is not very substantial. On the other hand, there is a sharp contrast with respect to other offices held (Table VI-F). Almost two-thirds of the rural legislators had been elected to other public offices, while only a little more than one-third of the urban legislators had been so elected. However, this urban-rural difference is slightly less than that shown, in the same table, to exist between Republicans and Democrats. Of course, about two-thirds of the Republicans are from rural districts, and about three-fourths of the Democrats from urban districts.

The offices to which Republican, and rural, legislators had been elected are mainly municipal (administrative and council), school board, and county board. Most of these offices were also heavily represented prior to 1957 in legislative biographies.[8] In 1957, eight rural legislators, all Republicans, were (or had been) not only county board members, but also county board chairmen. Simultaneously holding rural county board and legislative positions is common. This combination is important not only because it indicates the close tie of rural legislators to local political concerns, but also because it means that these legislators are likely to have experience, before coming to the state capital, in a parliamentary body somewhat similar in size to the legislature. Urban legislators do not always lack such experience, on municipal councils if not county boards. However, even municipal service appears to be more usual for legislators from smaller cities, many of which are here included in districts classified as rural. In particular, the large Milwaukee component of urban representatives does not recruit from county or municipal sources because the local Milwaukee positions, as already indicated, afford higher salaries than does the state legislature. In Milwaukee as well as in a few other large cities, simultaneous service on local councils and in the state legislature would be considered improper.

An interesting sidelight on the political experience of legislators is provided by the calculation, in Table VI-G, of legislators who had been defeated for public office (including previous tries for legislative office). Here, unlike the figures for *election* to other public office, there is no great difference between urban and rural legislators, or between Republicans and Democrats. However, what is discerned in comparing the two tables is that fewer rural and Republican legislators had been defeated than had been elected, while more urban and Democratic legislators had been defeated than had been elected. The explanations must be various. For example, more Democrats than Republicans had previously lost elections for state-wide and congressional offices; and some Milwaukee Democrats had tried without success to be elected to their county board or city council.

Education

As hypothesized, rural legislators have less formal education than urban legislators, but, as Table VI-H indicates, not much less. Much of the difference simply reflects the greater number of lawyers in the urban representation, and so a higher percentage of advanced degrees. The urban-rural difference is less apparent if all college and university degrees are considered together, instead of separating advanced degrees from undergraduate degrees. What then remains by way of an urban-rural differential is chiefly that a smaller percentage of urban legislators failed to complete high school. Interestingly, there is no such difference in educational levels when Republican and Democratic legislators are compared. However, the urban-rural contrast appears less significant than the over-all educational percentages indicating that less than half of the legislators had completed college.

Occupation

Data from the 1957 legislature do not establish any generally much greater portion of high-status occupations among urban than among rural legislators. The business-managerial category is about evenly represented—13 of the 61 rural legislators being so classified, and 10 of the 50 urban legislators. In the professional category, there is a disproportion, entirely on account of lawyers being more numerous in the urban delegation. Almost half (23) of the 50 urban legislators are lawyers, and only 17 of the 61 rural legislators. Even this difference, however, is not so great as to have any very definite significance when calculated for only a single legislature. As a group, lawyer-legislators have already been shown to share a characteristic, their relative youthfulness, which is more nearly uniform than their degree of urban concentration. In other than professional and business-managerial occupations, there is, as between urban and rural legislators, only the obvious point that farmers are from rural districts, and manual workers from urban districts.

The occupational classification of the 1957 Wisconsin legislators, shown in Table VI-A, may be compared with similar data on other legislatures although often systems of classification are not exactly the same. A 1949 tabulation of state legislators generally shows that 22.4 per cent were lawyers.[9] While this was somewhat lower than Wisconsin's percentage of lawyers as of 1957, the difference may reflect mainly a change over time, that is between 1949 and 1957. The percentage of lawyers in the Wisconsin legislature rose in the decade ending in 1957, coinciding with a decrease in the percentage of farmers.[10] A comparison of another type may be made to V. O. Key's tabulation, by party, of the occupations of Michigan and Pennsylvania legislators over four sessions.[11] In those two states, much more of the business-managerial category of legislators was Republican than Democratic, while almost all of the manual workers were Democrats. Although not presented here in tabular form, the Wisconsin data, when broken down by party, are roughly in accord with these tendencies.

Some attention should be devoted to a particularly interesting occupation, real estate and/or insurance, which is classified here and presumably in other tabulations either in the business-managerial or the sales-clerical category, depending on whether the legislator owned a business in which real estate or insurance, or both, were sold. A separate count of those in such a business, as owners or simply as salesmen, showed 13 in the 1957 Wisconsin legislature, and slightly more in the five previous legislatures. This may well involve an understatement since there are many classified in other occupations, particularly as lawyers, who are known to devote a substantial share of their time to real estate businesses. Generally it seems that real estate and insurance, like law, readily become part-time occupations and so are well suited for combination with legislative careers.[12] Also the gregarious nature of real estate and insurance salesmanship may be related to the qualities requisite for local political campaigns.

OCCUPATIONAL MOBILITY AND LAWYERS

As a socioeconomic characteristic of legislators, the degree of mobility has a special interest that makes separate consideration desirable. Concern is with the general hypothesis that American politicians are an upwardly mobile group. Admittedly, the test here of this hypothesis is very limited. The sole criterion of mobility is the legislator's occupation compared with that of his father, and data are confined to 105 members of the 1957 legislature who answered the particular questionnaire item about their fathers' occupations.[13] Therefore, such conclusions as emerge are highly tentative.

The hypothesis itself is stated in familiar form by the well-known American sociologist, Edward A. Shils: "In the United States politicians have an unusually high degree of social mobility. Politicians, more than any other profession, represent the realization of the idea of the poor boy who takes advantage of the opportunities of an open society and rises to the top. Even more than business men and intellectuals, American politicians have moved from the society of their birth and youth." [14] Since Shils made this statement with reference to legislators, it is especially pertinent to the present study even though his context was mainly congressional. As understood here, however, membership in the state legislature is not itself assumed to be a symbol of the arrival at the top by the upwardly mobile. Rather it is hypothesized simply that the legislature contains an upwardly mobile group, or, stated a little differently, that legislative membership is part of the career pattern of some upwardly mobile individuals. Unlike those in congressional or other higher political positions, state legislators have not, by virtue of their office, reached either a highly remunerative or highly prestigious goal. But many may be on their way to such a goal, and if they are it is reasonable to expect some of the ambition to be reflected in an already established higher occupational status than that of their fathers.[15]

Employing the same breakdown used in the previous section, Table VI-I shows the occupations of legislators and of the fathers of legislators. Immediately apparent are the larger percentage of legislators than of fathers in the legal profession, and the lower percentages of legislators than of fathers among manual workers and farmers. The difference within the business-managerial category is not so large, and in the case of non-legal professions—where the percentage of fathers is higher than that of legislators—the numbers are too small to permit of separate generalization. As between the political parties, the Republican legislators appear slightly more upwardly mobile by the criteria of their rise into the business-managerial class and their virtual absence in the manual-worker category. On the other hand, the drop in the percentage of farmers is not so sharp for Republican legislators vis-à-vis their fathers as it is for Democrats. The same broad patterns hold, as might have been expected, for the urban-rural comparison as for the Republican-Democratic. In both cases, the differences do not appear as significant (in Table VI-I) as does the common element of upward occupational mobility for legislators generally.

The most obvious feature of this mobility is the higher percentage of professionals (lumping together lawyers and other professionals) among legislators than among their fathers, and it deserves closer analysis. Of the 41 professionals among the 105 legislators, only 16 had fathers who were also professionals and only four had fathers who were in the business-managerial category. Of the remainder, 13 had farm backgrounds. In addition to the 16 professionals in the legislature whose fathers were also professionals, there were only three legislators who were not professionals although their fathers had been so, and two of these legislators were business-managers. Thus there is hardly anything that could be called a downwardly mobile group discernible here, while there can be little doubt in view of the number of professionals without professional or business-managerial family backgrounds, that there is a decided representation of the upwardly mobile. Since these professionals are mainly lawyers, plainly the legal profession is especially important in a study of occupational mobility of Wisconsin legislators, as indeed it is thought to be in studies of American politicians generally. Furthermore, the fact previously noted that lawyer-legislators are much younger, on the average, than other legislators makes it even more likely that upwardly mobile career patterns are to be found in this group.

Given the limited career possibilities of legislative service in and of itself, upwardly mobile young lawyers might be expected to limit their service to a relatively few terms before moving up to more remunerative public offices or moving out to full-time professional and business opportunities. Only in the early stages of a financially successful career would a lawyer usually find it financially advantageous to combine legislative membership with the maintenance of a law office. In line with this expectation, about two-thirds of the lawyers, compared to about half of the nonlawyers, in the 1957 legislature were in their first or second terms, and only one of the forty lawyers, compared to fifteen nonlawyers, had served as many as six terms. That these figures, indicating relatively brief legislative membership by lawyers, mean that lawyers do not usually want many terms is confirmed by interviews. Of course, lawyers are not alone in this respect, but the financial desirability of only limited legislative service seems especially characteristic of lawyers. As young men with a considerable investment in their own professional education, they are more likely not only to want higher political office but also to be interested in non-political economic advancement. As a group, the lawyer-legislators are distinctly on the make.

To find upwardly mobile men among lawyers, whether in politics or not, is hardly a novelty. Historically, as a leading legal scholar has pointed out, the American bar has been a middle- and upper-middle-class institution into which members of the lower-middle class have entered, and law has a "continuing role as one of the main roads of self-advancement for ambitious young men." [16]

An interesting question that remains is what sort of ambitious young lawyer enters the state legislature as a stage in his career, political or otherwise. That he is often without a family legal business to enter has already been indicated by the fact that most of the 1957 lawyer-legislators were not sons of lawyers. It would also seem likely that the young lawyer entering the legislature lacks the opportunity to join, and perhaps also the interest in joining, a large high-level firm where, given technical aptitude and application, he could secure substantial financial success. This is to say that the most proficient students of the law would less frequently turn up in the legislature than the ordinary students. Law teachers tend to confirm this in conversation on the subject, but always with the proviso that those who do enter the legislature may be very bright fellows even if their legal scholarship had been only ordinary. The matter has been tested in a laborious though not entirely adequate way. Of the 86 University of Wisconsin law graduates entering the legislature from 1909 through 1957, only four (or 4.7 per cent) had as law students attained the scholastic honorary society, Coif, which during this same period had admitted 11.3 per cent of all law graduates. The unavailability of similar data on graduates of Marquette University, the other major source of Wisconsin's lawyer-legislators, limits the scope of this study, but the University of Wisconsin figures alone are pretty convincing evidence that the best legal students less frequently enter the legislature than do other legal students. This does not necessarily mean that a smaller proportion of the best legal students enter politics generally. Instead of starting when young as state legislators, they may when older and established begin political careers at a higher level. In that case, however, as is often true of successful businessmen in politics, public office is less a step on a career ladder than it is a source of psychic satisfaction for a man who has already achieved material security.

Lawyer-legislators, almost from necessity, are in independent rather than salaried practice.[17] The attorney who, himself or in partnership, maintains his own practice is the one who enjoys the traditional possibility of engaging in politics as a part-time occupation. In this respect, the salaried lawyer is placed no more advantageously than any other salaried person. Also it might be noted that more of the independent than the salaried lawyers have very small incomes and so perhaps more of an economic incentive to gain legislative office.[18] The median income of Wisconsin lawyers in independent practice in 1954 was only $6,729,[19] so there were clearly many who had cause to supplement their legal incomes with legislative pay. This operates, it is fair to presume, especially in the early years of an independent legal practice.

Altogether it would seem that legislative membership suits the upwardly mobile young lawyer whose interest in his profession is less than the most scholarly or technical.[20] Emphasis is thus placed on the vocational career aspect of legislative service partly because of its connection to the analysis, in the next section, of postlegislative job opportunities. In the process of discussion, the usual reasons for lawyers in politics have thus been neglected. Some of these ought at least to be mentioned. Max Weber, for example, stressed the role of the lawyer in Occidental politics, since the rise of parties, as a response to the need for effective pleading of an interest group's cause in the same manner as a client's legal cause.[21] From a more strictly American view, attention has been directed to the naturalness of lawyers being called to legislative and other public responsibilities because of their skill in the accommodation of interests and in the adjustment of human relations.[22]

Acknowledgment of these legal attributes, complimentary or uncomplimentary, does not conflict with the premise of the earlier discussion. No matter how well-suited legal talents may be for the discharge of legislative duties, it is still reasonable to suppose that such talents would not usually be offered unless there were forseeable career advantages.

POSTLEGISLATIVE CAREERS

Since it is already clear that many members view their legislative service as only temporary, it is worth inquiring into the relation of such service to subsequent careers. This inquiry, as here conducted, is less relevant to the also substantial number of legislators who, typically elected for the first time as middle-aged or older men, do want to remain in the legislature for most of the rest of their active careers, or at least the rest of their political careers. This latter group, for whom legislative membership is politically terminal, has been readily distinguishable in interviews from the younger members who feel they cannot afford to stay in the legislature for many terms. The younger group, as previously emphasized, includes most of the lawyer-legislators, and may fairly be viewed as containing most of those who regard election to the legislature as some kind of beginning or intermediate stage in an upwardly mobile career.

By studying postlegislative careers, something may be learned indirectly about the career perceptions of legislators even though there is an obvious risk in seeing as goals what have turned out to be career results. The most conclusive way to demonstrate the nature of postlegislative careers would involve accounting for all of the activities of retired legislators over a period of several decades. However, that task would be prodigious in research time, and therefore only a very partial study has been conducted for the time being. Three aspects of postlegislative careers have been examined: election to higher office, losing candidacy for higher office, and work as a legislative lobbyist. As indicated in the previous paragraph, the scope is such as to relate much more probably to the subsequent careers of younger rather than of older legislators.

In dealing with political careers, it has to be recognized that the hierarchical order of offices may be entered at almost any place. There is no rigidity about advancement from lower to higher positions. Not only is there an absence of certain or even likely promotion for those entering near the bottom, but there is also no fixed barrier to one's initial political entry at a fairly high level.[23] For example, a prominent businessman may become governor, as has happened twice in the last two decades in Wisconsin, without ever having held previous public office. Thus state legislators in seeking to rise to higher offices must compete against outsiders as well as against others holding elected positions similarly situated fairly low in the hierarchy of public offices.

In this light, the number of legislators elected to higher office in Wisconsin, shown in Table VI-J, is fairly impressive. Between 1925 and 1955, almost one-third of the U.S. senators, governors, other state constitutional officers, and U.S. representatives (considered separately or together) were former state legislators.[24] Equally interesting are the facts, displayed in the same table, that those legislators who rose to higher office had been relatively young on entry to the legislature and had generally served rather few years. The exception to the latter generalization is provided by the legislators who subsequently became "other state constitutional officers," probably the least prestigious of the four higher categories.[25]

In contrast to the large proportion of ex-legislators in all four categories is the small number of ex-legislators holding elected judgeships in Wisconsin in 1955 (Table VI-K). Of course, the supreme court positions, elected on a state-wide basis, are difficult to attain, but the other judgeships are reasonably accessible and all are more attractive financially than legislative seats. On the other hand, a district attorney, among partisan officeholders, may be in a better position than a legislator to be elected judge, and, since judges are chosen on nonpartisan ballots at spring elections, a respected private attorney without strong party identification may be more advantageously situated than any partisan officeholder. At any rate, so few ex-legislators were judges in 1955 that it is hard to say that there is much of a career line from legislative to judicial office. Curiously, however, in 1957 two incumbent legislators became judges in their respective counties.

Returning to partisan offices, another calculation also reveals the extent to which legislators, and former legislators, seek higher political positions. This is a count not of how many were elected, but of how many lost (Table VI-L). In the same four categories of higher office used earlier, legislators and ex-legislators were numerous among both primary losers and general election losers in contests between 1924 and 1954. Percentages cannot meaningfully be calculated on the basis of the data given,[26] but the total of 98 legislators or ex-legislators who lost primaries and the total of 75 legislators or ex-legislators who lost general elections are impressive in view of the fact that there were only 254 elections (counting a primary and a general election for a given office as only one election). That there should, among legislators and ex-legislators, be many losing as well as winning candidates for Congress, in particular, seems natural. A congressional career would look attractive to one who had already learned something of legislative function and procedure, and a state senator especially would already have been elected from a constituency embracing nearly one-third of a congressional district. State senators, it should be added, have another advantage in that their four-year terms permit running for higher office every other time without surrendering their legislative seats. This is important to a politically ambitious legislator, for whom a seat may in itself have little value but for whom it serves as a useful springboard for future political moves.

Besides its relation to higher political office, legislative membership may serve also as a step in the kinds of careers that do not involve election campaigns. For instance, three majority-party legislative leaders were rewarded, within a four-year period, by gubernatorial appointment to full-time and high-level posts on state commissions. Nongovernmental career opportunities may also be promoted as a result of legislative experience. However, the importance of such experience to the strictly private income of ex-legislators, for example in legal practice, is ordinarily hard to measure. In the records of lobbyists, only the most obvious application of legislative experience to subsequent private gain may be studied. However, this is worth doing, and fortunately under Wisconsin's lobbyist-registration statute there are relatively complete records.[27] These registration records go back many years, but because a statutory change in 1947 had the effect of requiring only those lobbying for pay to register,[28] whereas until then many unpaid lobbyists registered as well, the records starting with the 1949 session are not comparable to those of earlier years.

For four regular legislative sessions beginning with that of 1949, Table VI-M shows the number of former legislators registered as lobbyists. Although there were never fewer than 18, and once as many as 24, these former legislators were not any large proportion of the total of between 200 and 300 registered lobbyists. This proportion may have the effect of understating the relative importance of ex-legislators among lobbyists. Many of the 200 to 300 lobbyists, even though all were working for hire, communicated only occasionally with legislators on one or two measures of interest to their clients. A minority could be counted as professional lobbyists, that is as men who spent most or all of the legislative session working in behalf of their clients' interests and who received large portions of their income for lobbying. Since these full-time legislative agents usually found it expedient to be generous providers of food and drink, as was legal through the 1957 session, they may be identified fairly well from their required reports of expenditures for entertaining legislators. Thus in the 1955 session there were 13 lobbyists who reported expenditures of over $1,000, and four of these were former legislators—all lawyers, incidentally.[29] Even this figure indicates that former legislators have nothing near a monopoly of the big-time lobbying role. More striking is a newspaper's tabulation showing that there were 10 former legislators among the 17 lawyer-lobbyists who in 1957 spent the most on food and drink for legislators.[30]

A different angle of approach to this same subject involves calculating the percentage of former legislators who subsequently became lobbyists. Of course, this tells one nothing about the degree of professional lobbying represented, but it does give a better idea of how many legislators subsequently assumed lobbying roles of some sort. The proportion, as shown in Table VI-N, is fairly high in general, but it is especially so for lawyers. Over one-third of the lawyers among legislators serving between 1919 and 1953 were registered lobbyists (as ex-legislators) at one time or another between 1921 and 1955. Clearly, as would have been expected, this is a much higher proportion than could hold for lawyers who had not served in the legislature. At the very least, then, lobbying, like running for higher partisan office, is a relatively significant postlegislative career possibility for a fairly well defined group in the state legislature.

SUMMARY

Despite the evident limitations of the data, in that they are derived from a single state and often from a single legislature, something may be said by way of summary concerning each of the hypotheses with which this chapter began. This is not to say that any hypotheses can be regarded as established or rejected generally for state legislators simply on the basis of Wisconsin findings.[31] At most this study might confirm certain propositions already widely accepted, but more likely what is said here needs to be tested elsewhere.

1) The status and salary of Wisconsin legislators have not been, and are probably not yet becoming, high enough to develop a full-time professional corps of legislators, and so to curtail the high rate of voluntary withdrawal found to be characteristic of state legislatures.

2) Urban legislators are younger than rural legislators, and they have less political experience as measured by other offices held. Their formal education and occupational classification differ mainly in that more urban legislators are lawyers. Except for strictly district residence, urban legislators appear to have as well-established local backgrounds as do rural legislators. Generally, it should be said that the urban-rural differences in socioeconomic characteristics were less sharp than had been supposed, and that they seemed overshadowed by common factors, especially the growing number of lawyers and the virtual absence of women in the legislature.

3) As measured by a comparison of the occupations of 1957 legislators with the occupations of their fathers, mobility from farm and manual-worker backgrounds to the law, in particular, is clearly discernible. As a group, in addition to being mobile in the way described, lawyer-legislators are also relatively young and urban, and especially likely, after membership of short duration, to move up or out in the interest of careers which appear to be more political or entrepreneurial in character than legal in a technical or scholarly sense.

4) Seeking higher partisan elective offices and becoming lobbyists, especially in the case of lawyers, are frequent enough among former legislators to indicate that legislative membership is an important step in such individual careers.

CHAPTER VII

Legislative elections

THE subject of this chapter is the process of legislative candidate selection, and this is interpreted to mean the conditions of selection as well as the selection itself. In studying the subject by an analysis of contemporary Wisconsin data, the following propositions are to be examined insofar as possible:

1) Even with equitable districting arrangements, the legislative representation of the state's traditional minority party has lagged behind the growth of that party's state-wide gubernatorial vote.

2) Legislative dominance by the traditional majority party has rested on small and medium-sized cities as well as on more rural areas.

3) Primary elections have substituted for general elections as a means of contesting legislative seats.

4) Primary elections have been causally related to the absence of two-party competition.

5) Organized parties have played a relatively small part in the selection of legislative candidates.

6) Campaigning for legislative office has tended to be highly personal.

These propositions, with the exception of the first two, center about the primary as a factor in candidate selection. The primary is explicitly stated as the focus of attention in the third and fourth propositions, and it is implicit in the fifth and sixth propositions. What is hypothesized is that the primary method of nomination stresses an individual as opposed to an organizational political style.

LAG IN MINORITY PARTY
REPRESENTATION

Wisconsin in 1946–1956 met two important conditions for service as a laboratory in which to examine the hypothesis that the legislative representation of the traditional minority party lags behind the growth of that party's share of the state-wide vote. First, Wisconsin Democrats were a growing minority party in the postwar decade, and second, the 1954 reapportionment established "one of the most representative lawmaking bodies in the nation." [1] The latter is particularly important because in so many other northern states a large share of the disproportion between the Democratic party's gubernatorial vote and its legislative membership is attributed to urban Democratic under-representation in one or both legislative houses. This factor may now be left out of account in Wisconsin. Such few districting inequities as exist, resulting mainly from a constitutional barrier against combining part of a county with another county (or with part of another county), do not add up to discrimination against urban areas.[2]

V. O. Key has stated the hypothesis plainly: "The data suggest that under American circumstances the weaker party—not simply the Democratic party—may be unable to build up its legislative strength as rapidly as its gubernatorial vote increases either in secular movement or through a stage of the political cycle." [3] Whether this implies something special about legislative as opposed to gubernatorial elections, which would not hold for lower relative to higher offices generally, constitutes a second interesting question. As Key has noted, a gap may also be discerned between presidential and gubernatorial voting in a given state, and between gubernatorial and minor state-wide offices.[4] Thus, in addressing the Wisconsin data, it is worth asking not only if there has been a lag in minority party legislative representation, but, if so, whether that lag is of a special kind because of the local nature of legislative election.

That there has been a lag in Wisconsin, conforming to Key's suggestion, is apparent from Figure 4, comparing the percentage of Assembly seats won by Democrats with the Democratic percentage of the gubernatorial vote, 1946–1956. The lag is per-

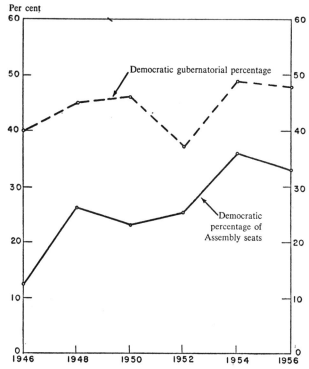

Figure 4.—Democratic Gubernatorial Percentage Compared with Democratic Percentage of Assembly Seats in Wisconsin, 1946–1956

sistent even though not quite so pronounced in 1954 and 1956 as it usually was during the earlier years of greater Democratic weakness as well as of malapportionment. An interesting feature of the record is that the lag operates when party fortunes decline as well as when they rise; thus the Democratic legislative percentage did not decline as sharply in 1952 as did the Democratic gubernatorial percentage. Even in 1952, however, the party had a much smaller share of the legislature than it had of the vote for governor. Of course, in no year, 1946 through 1956, were the consequences of the lag so significant as they would have been if the Democrats had won the governorship but not the legislature, thus dividing governmental responsibility with the Republicans. The possibility of this occurrence, even as soon as 1958 or 1960, cannot be dismissed.

In an effort to understand something of the nature of the lag, the situation in 1956 has been examined in another way. All of the votes cast for each party's Assembly candidates have been added, and then the respective Republican and Democratic percentages of the total have been calculated. The Democratic figure, compared to other relevant percentages, follows:

Democratic percentage of Assembly seats 33.0
Democratic percentage of total vote cast
    for all Assembly candidates 45.5
Democratic percentage of total vote cast
    for governor 48.1

From this comparison it is plain that the large gap between the Democratic percentage of Assembly seats and the Democratic gubernatorial percentage cannot be caused principally by there being fewer votes for the party's legislative candidates, in aggregate, than for the party's gubernatorial candidate. The fact is, as measured by the percentages above, that there are not so many fewer votes in the one case than in the other. Much of the explanation must lie in the location of the voters. Despite equitable reapportionment, Democratic voters have evidently not been so located as to elect the proportion of assemblymen to which their numbers would entitle them. Many of their ballots were wasted on a fairly small number of Democratic assemblymen with overwhelming majorities, greater in some districts than those of the Democratic gubernatorial candidate. Or, put the other way around, more Republican than Democratic assemblymen were elected from marginal districts.

Thus the Wisconsin findings, while not contrary to the hypothesis concerning the lag in the minority party's legislative representation, do indicate strongly that this particular kind of minority party lag represents more than a simple failure of voters to change their party allegiance as rapidly in the case of legislative candidates as in that of gubernatorial candidates. No doubt, that factor is present too, but it can account in the 1956 results for only about three percentage points of the fifteen-point gap between Democratic gubernatorial and Democratic legislative percentages. Those three points, incidentally, are about the same as the differential between the Democratic gubernatorial percentage and the lower percentage ordinarily polled by Democratic candidates for minor state-wide offices. It is the remainder of the gap that is to be accounted for by the special nature of legislative elections, and particularly by the uneven distribution of party voting strength among districts.

THE NATURE OF THE MAJORITY PARTY'S REPRESENTATION

In order to maintain its traditionally large legislative majority, Wisconsin's Republican party must include a heavy urban representation. If the U.S. Census terminology of urban and rural is adopted instead of that used in the preceding chapter (and elsewhere in this chapter), fewer than 50 per cent of the districts in each legislative chamber can be classified as rural, in the sense of having over half of their populations rural. As may be noted, however, from Table VII-A, the percentage of districts that are rural is slightly higher than the rural percentage (42.1) of the state's total population. Rural residents happen to dominate in a few, but only a few, more districts than their relative numbers in the state would justify. The important point remains that these rural districts are a minority in the legislature, and that only a few of the other districts, as may be seen in the same table, are as much as one-third rural. Another way of presenting Wisconsin's rural population as a minority with respect to legislative representation is to note that the 50 counties which voted against daylight-saving time in 1957 have only 37 of the Assembly's 100 seats, while the 21 counties voting for daylight saving have 63 seats.[5]

Even by the other urban-rural classification adopted especially for use in this work, any comfortable Republican majority has to have some urban members. That classification, which counted as rural all districts in which over half the population did not live in cities over 10,000 or in the large Census-defined urbanized areas, brings slightly more than half of the legislative seats into the rural category. The breakdown for each chamber may be seen in Table VII-B, where the urban districts are divided between metropolitan and smaller-city components. What is striking in this table is the more complete Republican dominance of the latter districts (characterized by cities of 10,000 to 50,000) than is true even of the rural districts. In the Assembly, the Republican-held rural seats are not quite numerous enough to provide a majority without some urban representation, drawn, as can be seen, more heavily from the districts of 10,000–50,000 population than from the larger number of metropolitan districts (where Republican strength is largely limited to suburban constituencies). The strength of the Republican party in the medium-sized cities is in sharpest contrast to the party's weakness in the metropolitan districts, which means principally in Milwaukee.

That the Republican majority has rested on some kind of urban base, though not on a metropolitan one, is even more evident when it is appreciated that many of the 53 Assembly seats and the 19 Senate seats classified as rural are but partly so by usual standards. Only seven Assembly seats and only one Senate seat have over half their populations living on farms. The remaining rural districts contain a mixture of rural non-farm and village populations along with cities under 10,000. The latter, that is the small cities, often bulk large enough so that Republicans must carry them in order to win the legislative districts involved.

It is Republican strength in small and medium-sized cities that enabled the party's large legislative majority to survive reapportionment in 1954 and 1956. Some of these places, along with suburban areas, gained representation as a result of re-districting in 1954, thereby compensating to some extent for the abolition of Republican rural seats. This may be observed in a close look at the first elections (1954 and 1956) following reapportionment. In the Assembly, 11 previously Republican rural districts had been eliminated (that is, merged with other districts), and of the subsequent 11 new districts the Republicans in 1954 managed to win five even though they were in urban areas. This was so in spite of the fact that 1954 was the peak Democratic year of the postwar decade, as measured by gubernatorial and legislative strength. In 1956 the Republicans did even better in the reapportioned Assembly districts, winning seven of the 11.[6] Of these seven, only one was a Milwaukee seat and two from other places over 50,000; the remaining four were districts dominated by cities in the small or medium-sized range. In the Senate, the results of reapportionment are more difficult to be precise about, although it seems doubtful that redistricting caused the Republicans to lose more than three Senate seats in 1954 and 1956. Generally what should be said about both houses is that the Republicans could have lost all of the new districts and still retained their legislative majorities (though not their useful two-thirds majorities), and that this is true because of Republican voting not only in heavily rural sections but also in those small cities which neither gained nor lost representation in the 1954 reapportionment.

Altogether, it is evident that the postwar legislative domination, just as the domination of other elected offices, by Wisconsin's traditional majority party has been linked to the special quality of the state's urban population which was stressed in Chapter Two. The state differs from many others in having a high percentage of its population in cities under 50,000 relative to the percentage in more metropolitan centers, and it is in the nonmetropolitan places that the Republicans preserved their traditional majority status. In this respect, as noted in Chapter Four, the postwar dominance of Republicans in Wisconsin may be a special case. Elsewhere there may not be the same population base, or the same kind of base, on which the traditional majority party can maintain its dominance.

On the other hand, one aspect of the composition of Wisconsin's legislative majority does resemble the situation in other northern states. The major metropolitan center, Milwaukee, is heavily underrepresented in the Republican party even though it is no longer so in the legislature as a whole. Republican legislators from Milwaukee have been scarce for many decades. Since 1932, only twice did Republicans comprise as much as half the Milwaukee delegation in the Assembly, and usually they were in a minority of between one-fourth and one-third. During this time Democrats, or Democrats and third-party Progressives, dominated the city's delegation.[7] Since reapportionment, the Democrats have held 20 of 24 Milwaukee Assembly seats in 1955, and 18 of 24 in 1957. It is not surprising, therefore, that Milwaukee legislators have occupied few positions of leadership in a Republican-dominated legislature. Taking both houses together, the handful of Milwaukee Republicans held one of 32 standing committee chairmanships in 1955, and one of 38 in 1957. During neither session, nor in any other recent session, was a Milwaukeean president pro tem of the Senate, speaker of the Assembly, or majority floor leader in either house.[8] Being thus largely removed from legislative leadership, and without sufficient numbers to be influential in the Republican legislative caucus, may have something to do with the sense of grievance maintained by the metropolitan center in relation to the legislature. Typical of this attitude is the summary of the work of the 1957 session appearing in Milwaukee's leading newspaper: ". . . city officials have expected so little from the legislature in recent years that a session in which the status quo is preserved is chalked up on the plus side." [9]

CONTESTS IN PRIMARIES AND
GENERAL ELECTIONS

Although Wisconsin appears to have established two-party competition in state-wide races, this hardly indicates that the pattern has been duplicated, at least in the postwar decade, in most legislative districts, or most counties. Through 1956, local elections implying the serious possibility of party changeover were decidedly exceptional. Where found, such two-party competition often existed only during a few years of transition from local dominance by one party to dominance by the other. Of course, it must be granted that the postwar decade provided fairly stable political circumstances so that, even with Democratic growth, there was no approximation to a revolutionary swing like that of 1932. Given some such development on a state-wide basis, it is fair to assume that there would be a chance for many more than the usual number of legislative seats to change hands at a general election. The most staggering possibilities were suggested by the results of the 1957 special senatorial election. In winning his substantial victory in a poll about two-thirds the usual off-year election total, the Democratic candidate had more votes than his Republican opponent in 82 of the state's 100 Assembly districts (only 33 of which were then held by Democrats) and 27 of the 33 Senate districts (only 10 of which were held by Democrats). The extent to which this special election result can be registered at a general election, and the extent to which it can there be reflected in legislative contests, will be tested in 1958. All that can be said here is that even the prospect of close general election competition would be novel for many districts.

This may be illustrated by the classification of districts shown in Table VII-C. On the basis of the 1956 election (in which the Republican-Democratic division of the state-wide gubernatorial vote was about 52 to 48 percent), there were 64 of the 100 Assembly districts in which a given party's Assembly *and* gubernatorial candidates won over 55 per cent of the vote. While these 64 districts are not all impregnably one-party, as the special election demonstrated, it is nevertheless true that 55 per cent majorities are ordinarily considered adequate for party safety. Here the measure is fortified by the requirement that the gubernatorial percentage as well as the assemblyman's percentage must have reached 55. This means that some Republican districts which would be counted as safe on the basis of an assemblyman's percentage are eliminated because the Democratic candidate for governor polled over 45 per cent of the vote in the district. Some Democratic districts in which the assemblyman won overwhelmingly are also eliminated from the "safe" category because in these the Democratic candidate for governor failed to poll over 55 per cent.

On the other hand, it should be noted that even if all of the plus-55 per cent districts were assumed to be noncompetitive, there remain enough Republican districts which, in a major party turnover, could give the Democrats a majority in the Assembly. In 1956, as shown in Table VII-C, Republicans held 16 seats with majorities for governor or assemblyman below 52 per cent, and 11 more between 52 and 55 per cent. Not all of these would have to be carried by Democrats to provide an Assembly majority. In fact, with the first 16 marginal seats added to the present Democratic strength of 33, only two of the 11 districts in the 52–55 per cent category would have to be won. This is possible in a Democratic swing considerably less drastic than that implied by the special senatorial victory of 1957. What this means, then, is that enough districts appear competitive in the 1956 tabulation to provide for two-party competition for Assembly control even though well over half of the districts may safely belong to a given party.

Instead of looking to future chances of two-party competition, it now seems more useful to measure the degree of party competition in a period for which the legislative election data are available. The simplest way to do this is to count the number of legislators defeated in general elections. Most striking in such a tabulation for 1946–1956 (Table VII-D) is that, besides the large number already noted as not seeking re-election, there were over twice as many defeated in primaries as in general elections.[10] In fact, the number losing in general elections is small by any comparison. Not only is it merely 14.3 per cent of all those not re-elected, but it is even less impressive as a percentage—5.2— of the total number (699) of Assembly and Senate elections, 1946–1956. Again, however, it must be said that these figures derive from an era without any drastic change in party fortunes. The year of greatest change was probably 1948, when the Democratic party at least established itself as a major force in state elections. This is reflected by more than the usual turnover at the general election of that year, as shown in Table VII-D.

The unusualness of serious two-party competition in the postwar decade makes the primary especially important to analyze as a substitute in providing voters with alternative candidates. Despite the fact that twice as many Wisconsin legislators were defeated for re-election in primaries as in general elections, there is still question about the adequacy of this method of competition. The question has previously been raised with reference to elections elsewhere, and particularly in an able critique of congressional elections by Julius Turner.[11] Concentrating on primaries in one-party districts, Turner found that there were few close contests and so not much by way of a realistic alternative to replace two-party competition. A priori, this finding with respect to congressional races, where the incumbency rate is high and admittedly a factor in limiting primary contests, might not be expected to hold for state legislative posts, where incumbency has already been shown to be low. However, the applicability of Turner's thesis to Wisconsin primaries ought to be explored in some detail. The same can be said for Key's propositions concerning primary competition for legislative offices in several states.[12]

The number of primary contests should be observed despite the limited importance of number alone as a criterion of the seriousness of contests. Eliminating only the obviously trivial candidacies, it is plain from Table VII-E that contested primaries are by no means universal. Just over half of the Republican and considerably less than half of the Democratic Assembly primaries, 1946–1956, were contested. By this standard, the voters were presented with alternatives in primaries less often than in general elections, where 85.5 per cent of the time the two parties at least presented opposing candidates, no matter how weak. One cannot help wondering how many of the remaining 14.5 per cent, without general election contests, were also without primary contests. That is, how many assemblymen were elected without competition either in the primary or the general election? As shown in Table VII-F, the numbers are not negligible. Forty out of 600 Assembly elections, 1946–1956, were decided without any contest at all, and this is an important portion of the 87 instances without general election contests. Primary contests thus often fail to appear in the very districts where one party is so weak that it does not even put up a candidate. Here voters have no choice to make at either election. That these are districts in which incumbents stand for re-election is shown decisively in Table VII-F. Furthermore, many of the same individuals are the uncontested incumbents over several elections. Yet, it may be granted, it is not unknown for these ordinarily secure incumbents to lose such primary contests as do, however rarely, occur.

Incumbency is not generally as much related to the absence of contests as might be suggested by the particular portion of cases cited above. In fact, as shown in Table VII-G, the relation is just the other way around in Democratic primaries. The percentage of primary contests is higher where there were Democratic incumbents. In Republican primaries, the percentage of contests is lower, but not much lower, where there were incumbents. As an explanation for this large number of primary contests against incumbents, Republican or Democratic, what occurs to the observer is simply that seats held by incumbents of a given party are going to appeal to others in the same party because these are likely to be the safe seats in general elections. Even though this explanation appears at odds with the previously demonstrated absence of contests in the very safest seats, it can be supported by some statistical evidence as well as by ordinary observation.

Here it is only necessary to confirm in Wisconsin the findings of V. O. Key for Indiana, and to do so the 1956 election data have been arranged in Table VII-H in the same form employed by Key.[13] It may be seen that generally the per cent of primary nominations which were contested increases along with the nominees' general election percentages, except where the general election percentages are 60 and over. This is the same general tendency revealed by Key, and even the tailing-off at the bottom of the table is in accord with his findings. The data substantiate his hypothesis that contested nominations are least likely where a party's cause is hopeless and most likely where a party has a large majority—but not one as large as 60 per cent or better.[14] This last proviso is a notable one, since it is established not only by the 1956 data of Table VII-H, but also by the absence of primary contests in almost half of the elections, 1946–1956, where the majority party was so strong there was no general election opposition at all (Tables VII-E and VII-F). In other words, in the extreme upper reaches of party strength the attractions of nomination do not produce contests so frequently as in the more moderately safe districts. Therefore, the incidence of primary contests is not solely a function of the size of the majority with which seats are held.

In seeking to explain the fall-off in frequency of primary contests at the highest levels of party strength, Key attributes some importance both to incumbency and to degree of urbanization.[15] The first of these factors has already been shown to have a most uncertain applicability to the Wisconsin phenomenon, since incumbency does not appear to be closely related to the absence of primary contests generally in Wisconsin. It is difficult to attribute major influence to the presence of incumbents in reducing the frequency of contests in the very safest districts when it does not do so for districts more uniformly.

Accordingly it may not be the presence of incumbents that causes the plus-60 per cent districts to have fewer primary contests; those districts may have certain characteristics which cause incumbents to seek re-election more often. One such characteristic might be urbanization, or rather the lack of it in the plus-60 per cent range of districts. This would be in line with Key's suggestion that there tends to be a higher incidence of primary competition in urban than in rural districts.[16] Accordingly, the Wisconsin districts in the plus-60 per cent range, where primary competition falls off, should be more rural than other districts. This turns out to be just barely true. Using U.S. Census definitions of *urban* and *rural,* in order to conform to Key's analysis, 25 of the 59 Assembly districts (Republican and Democratic), in which nominees polled over 60 per cent of the general election vote, had populations over half rural, compared to 40 of all 100 Assembly districts. More impressive is the fact that of the 59 districts a much smaller portion of the rural (9 of 25) than the urban (20 of 34) had contested primaries for the winning party's nomination. In short, there is some evidence for linking absence of competition to rural districts.

Returning to the broader problem of primary competition, the incidence of contests is also shown in relation to strong-Republican and strong-Democratic districts, as earlier classified according to the 55 per cent criterion in gubernatorial and Assembly elections. Table VII-I shows the percentage of primary contests to be markedly higher in a party's own strong districts and in its marginal districts than in districts strongly committed to the other party. Generally this is in line with the data of Table VII-H, although the breakdown is less fine. The absence of many Democratic primary contests in strong-Republican districts, and of Republican contests in strong-Democratic districts, is no more alarming than it is surprising. The primary adequately substitutes for general election competition by being used only where nominees have a chance of winning the general election.

Other factors, however, also relate to the adequacy of the primary as a substitute. One is the possibility of candidates winning primaries with pluralities short of half their party vote.

Since Wisconsin has no runoff requirement in any partisan primaries, the nomination of minority candidates is as distinctly possible for legislative as for state-wide office (see Chapter Three). Table VII-J shows that minority candidates did in fact win 152 Republican or Democratic Assembly primaries in the period 1946–1956. Furthermore, 118 of these nominees won the subsequent general elections and so served in the legislature as the choice of less than half of the majority party's voters in their respective districts. As the table indicates, these 118 minority choices amount to almost 20 per cent of the Assembly elections in the given period of time.

Another feature of the primary which has been subject to criticism, though from almost the opposite angle, is that there are few *real* contests among those contests appearing on the record. This was a major item in Turner's indictment of the primary as a substitute for the general election. Of the 965 safe-district congressional primaries which he examined, only 214 were decided by a margin of less than two to one.[17] Table VII-K shows that the proportion of close contests is much higher in Wisconsin's Assembly primaries (in all, not just in safe, districts, so the results are not truly comparable with Turner's). At least three-fourths of Democratic and Republican primaries in both 1954 and 1956 were decided by margins of less than two to one.

With this fact in the forefront, it is possible to reach the qualified conclusion that in Wisconsin legislative elections the primary does serve as a fairly adequate substitute for the general election. Primary contests are numerous as well as close, and although they are not so frequent as contests in general elections their use as a realistic substitute for the latter is apparent from their likelier presence in primaries where nomination probably, or at least possibly, means election. The qualification that must be reiterated is that there are fewer primary contests in the most strongly held seats than in those where majorities are only moderately strong, and that this holds for those seats which are so strongly held that there is no general election competition. The failure of the primary more frequently to serve as a substitute in these instances is serious since it means no contest at all. Less serious, though more usual as a qualification concerning the efficacy of the primary, is that it has resulted in numerous minority victories.

If Wisconsin's primary is more frequently contested in legislative elections than is true of primaries elsewhere, there are two special factors which may help to account for the phenomenon. First, the openness of the primary undoubtedly encourages contests especially at the local level because of the probability of attracting minority party voters into the majority party primary. Whatever the consequence for the doctrine of party responsibility, such a concentration of voters enhances the usefulness of the primary as a substitute for the general election in presenting a meaningful choice to the electorate.

Second, the present frequency of primary contests could be partly the result of Wisconsin's long experience with the primary, particularly in a former one-party situation where only primary contests were meaningful in state as well as in most local elections. Once established, it might be argued, the habit of locally contested primaries would continue even with the development of a two-party system on a state-wide basis. This possibility is supported by the record of Assembly primary contests from 1946 to 1956, the years in which the state changed in the direction of a two-party system. During this time, the number of Republican primary contests declined from 68 to 41, but the number of Democratic contests rose from 15 to 32; thus the net decline was only from 83 to 73. This preservation of primary contests coincides with the maintenance of mainly one-party districts despite the new two-party environment at the state level. But in 1956 there were fewer one-party Republican districts and more one-party Democratic districts than in 1946.

INFLUENCE OF THE PRIMARY IN
REDUCING TWO-PARTY COMPETITION

In the preceding section, the primary was discussed as though it were a device meant to compensate for the absence of competition in general elections, and no account was taken of the view that the existence of the primary is itself a cause of the absence of two-party competition. That view is tentatively advanced by V. O. Key, who believes that general election competition for state legislative seats is reduced by the effects of the direct primary on the vitality of local party leaders in minority situations. These leaders are thought less likely to produce attractive general election candidates, or any candidates, under a primary than under a convention system. Support for this belief Key infers from evidence of a greater diminution in general election competition in primary states than in Connecticut, which retained convention nominations.[18]

Causation in a complex matter such as this is hard to establish or refute. The difficulties are illustrated by subjecting Key's view to analysis in light of the Wisconsin data. Legislative seats uncontested in *general elections,* 1900–1956, have been tabulated in Table VII-L. The results are open to varying inferences. There were few uncontested seats before the primary took effect in 1906, and there were also very few in the succeeding decade. Any effects of the primary, it would have to be argued, were delayed, but this would seem only reasonable since it would take time for local minority party leadership to suffer from the atrophy attributed to the effects of the primary. After 1916 or so, unquestionably there was atrophy, from some cause or other, of the Democratic minority's leadership, state as well as local. This is reflected in the large number of uncontested legislative seats from 1918 through 1930, the heyday of Republican majorities and of primary battles between regulars and progressives. From 1932 through 1940, with either strong Democratic or third-party Progressive opposition, there were hardly any uncontested seats, but their number rose again with the decline and then the demise of the Progressives. Even in the recent two-party period, there have been a fair number of uncontested seats, some now Democratic instead of virtually all Republican seats as formerly. If only these recent years are compared with the era fifty years earlier, so as to have two periods when the two-party system prevailed, one might infer that the primary has reduced the number of legislative contests in general elections. However, the remainder of the table indicates so much movement that must be accounted for in other ways that it seems risky to attribute causation for any part of the change to the primary alone. Obviously the really large number of uncontested races of 1918–1930 cannot have been brought about solely, or even principally, because the primary caused local minority leadership to atrophy. If the primary were thus the cause, the local leadership should have stayed atrophied, as long as the primary remained, and there should have been no subsequent increase in two-party competition. Certainly there had to be other more important causes of change in party relations. By this reasoning, the most that might be inferred is that the primary was a minor cause.

Speculatively, however, it can be argued that the primary was an important factor in the original reduction of general election competition, and that the subsequent increase of competition, especially in recent postwar years, arose from new factors which even the effects of the primary could not suppress. Recent Wisconsin experience may fit the circumstances described by Key: "An increase, for example, in the effort devoted to the development and maintenance of a state-wide integrated party system might offset institutional depressants of party life that operate when such effort remains more or less constant." [19] That there has been strenuous party organizational work, stimulated from the center, is undoubtedly true of postwar Wisconsin, and it is fair to assume that such work stimulates minority candidacies for legislative positions in order to strengthen the party's state-wide ticket.

Such candidacies, while they afford the voter a general election choice where otherwise he would have none, may nevertheless be more nominal than real. Ticket-fillers are unlikely to be substantial or attractive candidates. Although such a matter is hard to measure precisely, since what makes for substance or attractiveness is problematical, something may be learned by looking at the occupational and educational levels of losing candidates. Fortunately the data on Milwaukee County candidates in 1956 happened to be readily available,[20] and these data serve the purpose at hand because about three-fourths of Milwaukee's 27 Senate and Assembly seats open in 1956 were won in the general election by 60 per cent or more of the total vote. Thus there are many instances in which a minority party must recruit candidates in a hopeless cause—in fact, so many were so hopeless that in seven districts there was no opposition party candidate in the general election. Among the 20 general election losers, only five were in professional or business-managerial occupations and only three had college degrees. This compares with 16 of 27 general election winners in professional and business-managerial occupations, and 14 of 27 with college degrees. Interestingly, those who lost in primaries, ordinarily of the majority party, also more often were of higher occupational status and had greater formal education than the general election losers. In short, when candidates are obtained by the minority party in Milwaukee County, even though it is the Republicans who are in this situation in most districts, the candidates appear to occupy less prestigious places in the community than the candidates of the majority party.

The obverse of this is that prestigious individuals seriously contemplating legislative election in safe districts seek the nomination of the majority party. But this is not to say that they are more likely to do so, rather than competing as minority party candidates in the general election, *because* there is a primary rather than a convention system. Strong minority party candidates might be as hard to come by under one system as another. Again it is hard to attribute minority party problems to the primary.

PARTY FUNCTIONS

While the effects of the primary, as opposed to the convention system, on party recruitment of candidates cannot be satisfactorily measured by data available in this study, there remains the possibility of learning more about party functions with respect to legislative elections in the present institutional environment. Since that environment is indeed characterized by the open primary, whatever is learned may have some relevance to the general problem previously discussed but, to repeat, causation cannot thus be established.

Party, in this discussion as in most of this work, refers to the voluntary and extralegal organizations described in Chapter Five. The law effectively prevents the skeletal formal parties from doing any more than accepting nominations made by primary voters. And whatever control the voluntary organizations—that is, the actual parties—exercise over nominations is of a sort unrecognized by statute. Their endorsement of candidates before a primary is a private affair, and here it is important to note again that endorsement is rare in the case of legislative or other local offices. Only a few local Republican units have gone so far in the direction of a formal commitment to a candidate. This means that an inquiry into the function of parties in legislative elections must, insofar as it concerns candidate selection, be an inquiry into informal practices. The only way to learn of these practices is to ask the politicians themselves. In part, this was done in the questionnaires sent to party officers and used extensively in Chapter Five; where the data from those questionnaires are relevant to the present purpose, they will be referred to again. Also the previously mentioned field studies in selected counties provided some answers to this particular inquiry, but attention here will be focussed on the answers given by the 111 legislators who responded to the appropriate items of their questionnaires.

An indirect way of approaching the question of the party's relative importance in legislative elections is to learn the extent to which successful candidates had been party activists. In other words, are legislators party men? Of course, all may be assumed to claim party membership in some sense of that vague term. Table VII-M shows the number of years of membership. The fact that many, particularly among the Democratic legislators, have been members for less than ten years does not signify that they are necessarily "Johnnie-come-latelys." Youth accounts for some of the recentness of Republican and Democratic membership, and the newness of the Democratic organization accounts for more of the Democratic legislators. However, nothing in this table indicates positively that long party faithfulness accompanies legislative election. Neither is there anything in the record of party activity, as revealed in Table VII-N, to give such a positive indication. Only about half the legislators had held any office in their party organizations, and since "offices" include a great many committee chairmanships as well as the usual presidency, vice-presidency, and secretaryship, the record is not very impressive. In the vaguer category of "other activity," there were more affirmative answers but these could refer to very slight activity indeed. It would seem that any legislator at all prominent in his local organization would have had some kind of office at one time or another. The percentage who did hold party offices, it should be observed from Table VII-N, was higher among Democrats than Republicans, and among urban than rural legislators. Especially in the case of the latter comparison, this reflects what was established in the earlier discussion of parties: their greater role in urban areas. Generally in urban as in rural areas, however, what is indicated by the data on legislators' party activity is that it is distinctly possible to become a public office-holder in Wisconsin without observing the old adage about the need to start as a precinct committeeman and work one's way up the party ladder. Nominal party membership often seems sufficient.

The most significant index of party function in legislative elections is its influence in the nominating process. Replies from legislators, when the subject was raised directly (Table VII-O), lead one to believe that influence to be slight. Over half of the legislators reported that they won their original nominations when party leaders either favored another candidate, took no action at all, or were divided. In only 13.5 per cent of the cases did legislators report that party leaders persuaded them to run. Twenty-seven per cent reported merely encouragement. These results are fairly uniform as between strong-party and competitive districts, although more positive party action is reported in strong-Democratic districts than elsewhere.[21] Much the same general finding is apparent in tabulating the results of the question of how legislators happened first to be interested in running for their present positions (Table VII-P). One-fifth credited party leaders with originally suggesting that they run. While this proportion, like that reported in the preceding tabulation, does indicate some party leadership activity, perhaps more than in many other states, it still represents a distinct minority of cases.

It might be argued that legislators understate the role of party leaders in order to emphasize their own personalities and accomplishments. If so, legislative responses would be at odds with those of party officers reported in Chapter Five. This does not appear to be the case, but it may be admitted that no exact comparison is possible. Much of the activity concerning legislative nominations which party officers reported was in districts which were lost (by the party of the officers reporting), and so did not affect the nominations of the winning legislative candidates. In any event, however, most party officers claimed no more activity than encouraging, seeking, or persuading (in that order) candidates to run, and their emphasis particularly on encouraging candidacies is consistent with the reports of legislators. Despite their evident usefulness in filling the ticket in apparently hopeless districts, party officers otherwise asserted no strong influence in the nominating process.

Parenthetically, it may be observed that the limited role of parties in primaries is partly paralleled in general election campaigns. Unlike the situation in the primary, there is no question about the propriety in a general election of formal party commitment to a candidacy. Even so, there have been only limited efforts by state party organizations to promote their nominated legislative candidates.[22] Local party efforts have been uneven, although, as shown in Table VII-Q, about four-fifths of the legislators acknowledge either some or considerable help in general election campaigns from their local party organizations. Surprisingly, the proportion is no higher in competitive districts than in strongly held districts. "Some help" is more frequent in the competitive districts, but "considerable help" less frequent. And it should be emphasized that reporting "some help" meant that the legislator checked the choice which read "some help but not of great importance in my campaign." Thus only the choice of "considerable help" indicated that the legislator viewed his local party organization's help as of any real importance. Just about one-third of all legislators, and but one-fourth of the legislators from competitive districts, are in this category.

On the other hand, it may be assumed that the party label, in contrast to the party organization, is important to virtually all candidates. In most districts, a given party label is *the* means by which one gets elected. The point is that this label is won in the nominating process which, the evidence indicates, is not controlled, or usually decisively influenced, by the party organization. The evidence presented, it may be granted, is not conclusive, but this is the place to stress that such field studies as have been conducted tend to confirm the general impression of limited organization influence.

The relevance of this situation to attempts to maintain party discipline and cohesion among legislators is worth discussing. Such attempts, incidentally, have been fairly successful in Wisconsin. In the postwar decade both houses were regularly organized by the Republican majority, and while party lines often broke on particular issues the most significant business of each session, particularly the budget, was firmly controlled by the majority caucuses operating under party leadership.[23] The fact that legislators have so largely been selected by nonparty influences does not, apparently, prevent their functioning for many important purposes as party members in the body to which they have been elected. Although virtually autonomous, the legislative parties have become effective. But is it likely, as orthodox doctrine holds, that the legislators would function still more fully and faithfully as legislative party members if they owed their nominations to party organizations? The answer would seem to be negative where organizations were locally oriented and controlled. Such organizations would represent but another local pressure (and probably an especially strong one) to prompt a legislator occasionally to desert his state-wide legislative leadership. On the other hand, influence in the nominating process by a central state organization would presumably contribute to legislative party cohesion. At least, that would be its purpose.

Party organization influence, as studied here, appears to be of a character in between the purely local and the central authority. The leaders involved are local party officials, but they tend, as shown in Chapter Five, to be oriented toward state and national issues. Although it is thus by no means certain what effect an increased organizational influence would have on legislative behavior in Wisconsin, the state-wide party ties of the local leaders would seem more likely to make the organization's function, when exercised, centripetal in its impact on a legislative party.

PERSONAL CAMPAIGNING

With party organizations decidedly limited in influencing legislative elections, the style of campaigning actually used becomes of considerable interest. What is being asked about here, it must be borne in mind, is the primary election campaign at least as often as the general election, because of the already demonstrated frequency with which primary nomination means safe election.

While it is hypothesized that campaign style in this situation tends to be highly personal, this does not mean that nonparty groups are entirely out of the picture. As indicated by Table VII-R, presenting legislators' answers to a question asking which group had usually been of greatest help in their campaigns, a number of groups besides party organizations are considered important by legislators. These are county board memberships (chiefly named by Republicans), unions (named almost entirely by Democrats), and farm organizations. Equally noteworthy is the frequent dismissal by Republicans of the question by naming only "friends" or "none."

More directly pertinent to the style of campaigning are the results of the question asking legislators to check the methods they used when first elected (Table VII-S). The most striking feature is that over half of the legislators used the door-to-door technique. The frequent use of flyers, pamphlets, and matches is of a piece with this intensely personal campaign style, and so is the often acknowledged help of family and friends. The limited use, as expected, of radio and television reflects the small-scale, local level of office, for which expensive communication media are ordinarily unsuitable. Small local stations, where rates are low, constitute the exception. Newspaper advertising, as may be noted, is used widely, although less in urban than in rural districts because space in metropolitan papers is prohibitively expensive. Generally candidates are encouraged to run newspaper advertisements because the cost of one quarter-page in each newspaper in the district (along with one mailing of literature) is excluded from statutory limits of expenditure. These limits—$1,000 for a senator and $400 for an assemblyman [24]— can, of course, be circumvented by the establishment of voluntary committees, but these are unusual in the case of legislative candidates. Their campaigns are still pretty modest, and they tend to be conducted by the candidates themselves rather than by committees. The biggest expenditure is of the candidate's own time, especially if he conducts a door-to-door campaign.

The personal element may again be shown by the fairly low frequency with which party organizational help is reported among legislators' campaign methods. Conforming to previous tables, hardly more than one-quarter of the legislators acknowledge such help even along with other items. However, it ought to be said that from this or any other tabulation it is hard to convey the style of campaigning that characterizes legislative elections. Field study has provided more of the flavor of the personal political style.

SUMMARY

Although already having confessed to frustration in dealing with some of the most interesting hypotheses with which this chapter began, I believe that a summary of findings is in order.

1) Despite equitable reapportionment, the legislative representation of the state's minority party has lagged decidedly behind that party's state-wide gubernatorial vote, and the lag has been greater than that indicated by the total vote for all of the party's candidates for the Assembly.

2) The traditionally dominant party, Republican as elsewhere in this region of the United States, maintained its large legislative majority through 1957 by strong representation not only from rural areas but also from small and medium-sized cities. This is more feasible in Wisconsin than in states whose urban populations are more heavily metropolitan.

3) With some important qualifications, the primary has substituted for the general election in providing legislative contests in the state's numerous districts which have been dominated by a single party. Insofar as the primary in Wisconsin, at least in legislative elections, has thus been used more than elsewhere, the explanation may lie in its openness and in its long history.

4) The primary as a cause of the absence of effective two-party competition for legislative seats is neither proved nor rejected on the basis of the Wisconsin data presented. It is granted that the primary limits party organizational control of nominations and opens another channel of competition, which are what the primary is supposed to do, but it is uncertain that without these consequences there would have been more serious general election competition.

5) Views of legislators, supported by field observation, confirm for Wisconsin the general view, indicated above, of a limited party organizational influence in the selection of legislators, particularly of legislative candidates in primaries.

6) Consistent with the limited organization role is the evidence of a strongly personal style of campaigning.

Generally with respect to the broadly hypothesized influence of the primary method of nomination, the findings concerning Wisconsin legislative elections provide no basis for dissenting from Key's view that "the new channels to power" represented by the primary "placed a premium on individualistic politics rather than on the collaborative politics of party." [25] What evidence there is in this chapter is of relatively individualistic politics, and of a sort consistent with the primary method of nomination. However, no case whatsoever is made out for these individualistic politics being caused by the existence of the primary. It is just as reasonable to suppose that the primary itself is the result of individualistic politics, and that the institution is adapted to these politics rather than the politics to the institution.

CHAPTER VIII

Speculative implications

A GRAND summary of findings is unnecessary. Each chapter of this study contains its own summary, and no useful purpose would be served by bringing all of these together in one list. Instead this concluding chapter is reserved mainly for speculation on the meaning of some of the principal findings already reported. Here, it must be confessed, the intention is to discuss implications which the Wisconsin data merely suggest but do not support. No longer is the deliberate effort to be made, as it was in the bulk of this work, to confine observation to highly specific matters. The scope of this concluding commentary is less limited. The meaning of the Wisconsin findings for an understanding of state politics generally is now of prime concern, and along with this concern goes an interest in future research which might test the speculative implications noted here.

It is useful to center speculation about the extent to which Wisconsin politics approach the democratic political model of highly organized state and national two-party competition. As indicated in the introductory chapter, such a model served loosely as the source for many hypotheses presented in the course of the study. Wisconsin data have thus been employed to test a theory of politics designed to apply to the United States generally, and whatever broad tendencies are observed here might be readily related to the study of the political experience of other states.

Initially the matter of party competition may be considered

apart from organizational developments. In simple electoral terms, there is no doubt that Wisconsin politics of the postwar decade came to be based on a Republican-Democratic competition in general conformity with the national alignment. By this transfer of the state's customary conservative-versus-progressive contests from the Republican primary, after a transitional third-party period, to the general election between Republicans and Democrats, Wisconsin may be said to have responded to essentially national forces. The most usual explanation for the change to two-party politics is that the state, like others in the north-central region, could maintain its one-party Republicanism only as long as national elections were fought largely along sectional lines. When, it is argued, American politics became effectively nationalized (at least outside the South) by the issues of the New Deal era, contests between Republicans and Democrats became viable where they had not been so before.[1] In other words, as a truly national party, rather than a sectional party, the Democrats could offer substantial competition in Wisconsin, and furthermore, it is contended, they almost inevitably would do so because of the importance of the new national issues to voters in Wisconsin as elsewhere.

Compatible with this line of explanation is the fact that Wisconsin's old one-party system did not break down for any apparent internal reasons. Republican primary contests had provided genuine electoral competition from 1906 through 1932, when voters were usually presented with a choice between candidates of recognizable conservative and progressive factions. What caused the system to collapse in the 1930's was the drift of progressive voters to the Rooseveltian Democratic party, which drift the La Follettes could halt only temporarily at the state level by establishing a third party. And what prevented the effective re-establishment of intra-Republican competition in the postwar period was the unwillingness of enough nationally oriented Democratic voters to follow the La Follettes back into the Republican primary. The national pattern, derived from the New Deal period, finally imposed itself on Wisconsin politics after World War II. The delay, relative to other states, can readily be attributed to Wisconsin's particularly long and successful progressive-conservative competition outside the two-party arena. The stronger the old system, the longer the period of transition to the new.

Another possible cause for the delayed development, even in the postwar period, of an effective Democratic opposition may lie, as suggested in earlier parts of this work, in the distribution of the state's population. In a period when Democratic votes have been drawn heavily from metropolitan centers, it is especially relevant that a smaller proportion of Wisconsin's population lives in a single metropolitan center than is the case in many other states of the region. The importance politically of this distribution is apparent from the fact that medium-sized cities, even up to 50,000, did not usually produce Democratic majorities in postwar Wisconsin politics. Along with the numerous smaller cities and villages, the medium-sized places remained regularly Republican during the first decade of two-party competition. Until 1957 this was enough to offset Democratic metropolitan majorities as well as the changeable character of much of the declining farm vote.

However, Democratic victories in the future are not entirely dependent on the likely growth in metropolitan population. As was shown by the special senatorial election of Proxmire in 1957, a Democratic state-wide candidate can in favorable circumstances win majorities in the medium-sized cities as well as in the larger centers and the farm townships. Perhaps this requires, especially if majorities are also to be extended to small cities and villages, that Wisconsin Democrats modify the national image of their party. In an environment that remains largely nonmetropolitan, a party oriented toward voters in large cities may be at some disadvantage—though less so in Wisconsin than in the even less metropolitan states farther west. Nationalization of politics, without defeating itself, cannot be carried so far as to eliminate a party's appeal to a given state for the sake of conformity to the national cause. Democratic party identification with big cities and big unions, not to mention big international expenditures, is not everywhere the formula for political success. This formula has already been modified by Wisconsin Democrats, notably in the successful efforts of Proxmire and others to win the farm vote but also in appealing to small businessmen. By adding the changeable farm vote, in particular, to the labor union votes of urban communities, the Democratic party's combination resembles that of the formerly successful Progressives except that, in keeping with the changed character of the state, the urban proportion is now much higher.

Apart from Wisconsin's population distribution, there are special and less fundamental factors to help account for the politics of the postwar decade. One of these factors involves the timing of national voting trends. In 1948, when there was a moderate Democratic trend reflected in elections nationally, Wisconsin Democrats were still too new and little-known to benefit materially even from Truman's majority in Wisconsin. Afterward the state party and its candidates were in an apparently better position, but the presidential elections of 1952 and 1956 hardly provided any coattails for state Democratic candidates. In fact, by 1956 the Democratic gubernatorial candidate in particular was strong enough to run well ahead of Adlai Stevenson. Given these accidents of timing, Democratic victories in Wisconsin would have required especially fortunate local circumstances, such as major scandals in state Republican administrations, and these were not provided. In other words, nothing occurred between 1946 and 1956 to shake the usual Republican voting pattern in state elections.

Here it seems relevant to note that when a Democrat did finally win major state-wide office in 1957 the occasion was a special election to fill a U.S. Senate vacancy. With no other offices subject to simultaneous election and therefore no party ticket loaded with well-known local Republican officeholders, it may be speculated that the old pattern is more readily broken. Such also seems to be the lesson of Democratic success in the special election of 1953 in the previously Republican ninth congressional district. What is suggested by these results is that a breakthrough by candidates of a minority party does require some kind of special circumstance, if not that of a national landslide or a highly dramatic state issue, at least of an unusual election procedure. Once elected in any such circumstance, no matter how special, the victorious candidate possesses advantages of incumbency which may enable him, and his party, to capitalize on the original breakthrough. This is not to say that such capitalization of success, or even the breakthrough itself, could be achieved without simultaneously favorable opportunities created by national trends. Broadly, as already indicated, such trends appear responsible for the postwar development of two-party competition in Wisconsin, and it is only the incidence of minority party success in this competition which needs to be explained by special circumstances.

Based on experience in other states, the Wisconsin Democratic party, if and when it does achieve success in a general election (for instance, in 1958 or 1960), might be expected to win only partial control of the state government. Elsewhere, at any rate, the initial victories of a traditional minority party have often been limited to top state offices, leaving one or both houses in the hands of the old majority party. The division of executive and legislative powers, in this manner, between the two parties is likely in Wisconsin even though both the state Senate and the Assembly are equitably apportioned. That is, it is likely when a minority party is becoming a majority, or of course at any time when the two parties are closely matched, but not, as it is in many states, as a permanent result of discriminatory districting arrangements. Thus in the Wisconsin Senate a party turnover is difficult to achieve in a single election simply because either 16 or 17 members are holdovers. And even in the Assembly, where the whole membership is elected every two years, it cannot be assumed that the traditional minority party would win control the first time it won the governorship. As described in Chapter Seven, there has been an appreciable gap between the percentage of votes cast for the Democratic candidate for governor and the percentage of Democrats elected to the Assembly. Whether this gap would be maintained sufficiently, if at all, in a year of general Democratic victory so as to prevent Democratic control of the Assembly, cannot, obviously, be confidently answered in advance. Among other things, the answer depends on the size of any state-wide Democratic majority and on the extent to which state-wide victory was anticipated so as to have brought forth stronger than usual legislative candidates on the Democratic ticket.

Serious two-party rivalry in Wisconsin, it should be stressed, has been presented mainly in terms of state-wide political power. In this as in other analyses of state politics, conformity to the competitive model often seems to be based only on contests, like those for governor and U.S. senator, which measure party strength in the state as a whole. Similarly even when respective party membership in the state legislature is weighed, it is over-all state strength which is of concern. What is disregarded is the degree of two-party competition which may or may not exist at the local level—for example, within counties, legislative districts, or even sections of the state. A serious rivalry of Republicans and Democrats for state-wide offices, or for majority control of the legislature, need not be based on any close approximation to an even distribution of Republican and Democratic voters over the state. Local one-party dominance is compatible with state-wide two-party competition as long as each of the two parties dominates in areas of roughly equal population. Serious local contests between the two parties can be few, or almost nonexistent, and yet the state as a whole be fairly evenly divided.

That Wisconsin's postwar two-party competition approximated this condition seems evident, especially in light of the one-party dominance of legislative districts. Not only was Republican monopoly maintained in many communities, but especially in metropolitan districts the Democrats established a dominance of their own. Some areas did change from Republican to Democratic officeholders during the growth of the Democratic party, and briefly appeared to have two-party competition. However, serious two-party competition in local elections has seldom been sustained. Even in a metropolitan area, where some party competition may exist at the county level, most of the several legislative districts of the area have been likely to belong overwhelmingly to one party or the other.[2]

Some such pattern of localized party strengths underlying state-wide competition is so common that it could be superfluous to describe it. In this respect, Wisconsin obviously resembles many other states, and other countries for that matter. Everywhere the two-party system, when based on geographical representation, functions with each party having its own areas of nearly absolute dominance, and thus always some representation in the legislature despite a landslide election victory for the opposition. This, it may be argued, is itself useful to the maintenance of continued state-wide competition since the minority draws some of its leadership in future elections from the ranks of those elected in safe districts and, in addition, needs a legislative delegation in order to function as a critic of the majority party. What are conceived, then, as the advantages of the two-party competitive model must be fulfilled by a statewide choice, in effect, of one legislative party or the other, without a universality of serious local contests.

Nevertheless a state-wide rivalry is supposed to stimulate local rivalries, just as national two-party competition is supposed to have affected state-level politics. In a limited way, at least, this did occur in Wisconsin's postwar politics. The development of Democratic competition for state offices encouraged local Democratic candidacies, even in hopeless districts, in order to fill the party ticket and so improve the party vote for higher offices, but as long as such minority candidacies were hopeless, or nearly so, the advantages of two-party competition at the local level were not really achieved. It is hard to say at what point the hopeless character ends and the local general election thereby becomes significant. No doubt, this point could be reached in 1958 in some of Wisconsin's previously safe Republican districts because of Senator Proxmire's special senatorial election victory in such districts. Even in districts dominated by small cities and villages, the monopoly of respectability previously held by the one-party Republican tradition might be broken by the entry of impressive Democratic candidates. Whether, however, this encouragement of substantial Democratic opposition would mean a net gain in the number of two-party competitive localities remains uncertain. The same factors encouraging serious Democratic candidacies in Republican districts might discourage serious Republican candidacies in Democratic districts. Democratic optimism is likely to coincide with Republican pessimism.

What this discussion implies is a considerable skepticism about the "normality" of two-party competition at a level like that of Wisconsin's legislative districts, or of most of the state's counties. Such skepticism, it is granted, does not rest on conclusive evidence. Although observation of Wisconsin politics in the postwar decade reveals very few stable local two-party situations, these may yet develop in response to a longer-lived state rivalry between Republicans and Democrats. On the other hand, no such development can be assumed on the basis of the experience of other states. Those states with two-party competitive systems of long standing are not characterized by relatively even geographic distributions of party voters. The same can be said of Britain despite that country's highly developed party system. Indeed one-party dominance of numerous areas appears to be the norm within a larger jurisdiction where two-party competition prevails.

In Wisconsin, historically, competition in the primary of the local majority party tended to substitute for the absent two-party competition. This uniquely American election device, most highly developed in Wisconsin, thus provided voters a meaningful local choice where otherwise, because of their commitment to a given party, they would have had none. As evidenced by state legislative elections in the postwar decade, local primary competition continued to be significantly frequent even though the relative importance of the state-wide primary greatly declined during the period. However, the nature of legislative primary contests after 1946 differed sharply from those of the old progressive-conservative rivalry of the Republican party, 1906–1932. Now contests were not so overwhelmingly within the Republican party, and they were not between candidates, local and state, of recognizable factions. Their ideological significance, then, seems to have been reduced, but the habit of competing and voting within the majority party, whichever one it happens to be, remains firm, so far at any rate, despite state-wide two-party rivalry.

This leads to the question of what effect the abolition of primaries would have on two-party competition. Since primaries do provide an alternative means of electoral competition, it can be argued that their abolition would channel opposition into the minority party since it could no longer be expressed electorally within the majority party. Thus, the argument continues, two-party competition would be strengthened locally as well as at other levels. This assumes that the creation of primaries in the early 1900's tended to lessen what two-party rivalry then existed, as well as to inhibit its subsequent development. However, Wisconsin's historical experience, as presented in Chapter Seven, does not adequately support this assumption, and it is entirely plausible to understand the state's development of the open primary as a response to a one-party situation rather than as the cause of it. Furthermore the continued existence of the open primary in the postwar years did not prevent the growth of two-party competition for state-wide offices. Why should it be held to prevent the growth of such competition at the local level? Surely it is reasonable to believe that local one-party dominance would also prevail without the primary, as it does elsewhere in the world. In that case, much can be said on behalf of the primary, especially in its open form, as a means by which voters can exercise a choice in the election of candidates.

Although meeting the criterion of meaningful electoral competition, as established by the democratic model, the Wisconsin primary, it is true, now serves a more limited purpose than it did in the days when the state as a whole, not just localities, had a one-party character. Then the primary was the decisive arena of policy choice between progressives and conservatives, both in state-wide and in legislative contests. Now, with a few important exceptions, the general election has become the place for voters to register their preferences on broad policy questions. What is left for voters in primaries is largely to choose between rival personalities, in state-wide races and especially in legislative contests. The primary still provides an opportunity for competition, but mainly for competition of a different kind from that of the early twentieth century intra-Republican contests and from that of the postwar general elections.

This suggests, however, a continuity in Wisconsin electoral competition between the old Republican intraparty contests and the present two-party rivalry. Differences over policy between the old progressives and stalwarts are paralleled by many of the latter-day differences between Democrats and Republicans. The division of the electorate remains basically similar even though the decisive contests have shifted from primary to general election, and despite important changes in the character of the voting population. In this perspective, the development of a postwar two-party system, as described in Chapter Three, remains novel in form, and sufficiently so as to explain many obstacles in the way of Democratic party success. Nevertheless, in substance, an electoral bipolarization over Wisconsin policy questions is traditional.

So far in discussing the two-party model, the matter of party organization has been kept to one side. However, the belief that parties should be highly organized is as much a part of the model as is the belief in two-party competition. The image ordinarily conveyed is of parties devoted to programs and policies of their respective memberships, and thus of parties sufficiently organized to have numerous articulate memberships. This does not mean that elected candidates are always envisioned as responsible only to their parties, rather than to the larger number of voters. However, at the very least it does mean responsibility to a party program presented as such to the electorate by, or in behalf of, an organized membership. It is this aspect of the model which political scientists have usually found missing in the United States even when electoral competition is plainly conducted between candidates of two parties engaged in fairly even rivalry. In other words, American parties have appeared loose, uncohesive, and relatively uncommitted to specific programs or policies. These attributes have been associated with the absence of large dues-paying memberships, either as cause or effect.

In this frame of reference, the development of organized party membership in Wisconsin has been explored in some detail in this work. Such organization has progressed, at least in urban and middle-class areas, to the point of providing fairly numerous activists engaged in party tasks on a regularized basis. Not the least of these tasks has been to secure candidates for apparently hopeless local races. Even if a great deal of political activity remains outside this organizational sphere, especially in personal campaign committees and in labor union get-out-the-vote drives in industrial working-class districts, the Wisconsin parties are now much more than skeletal in character. The orientation of their memberships is largely around national and state issues, and on these issues there appears to be a fairly clear-cut distinction between Republicans and Democrats.

Whether these party organizations have succeeded, or can succeed, in establishing the "responsibility" of candidates, as prescribed by the model, is open to question. Of course, such responsibility may to some extent be achieved regardless of the degree of party organization provided the voters of a given party are sufficiently conscious of policy questions. Organizational influence, as such, is obviously limited by the inability of a Wisconsin party to control its party label. Candidates can in theory and occasionally in practice win primary nominations against the desires of the organized membership of the party which they then represent on the general election ballot. The substantial organizational efforts of Wisconsin Republicans to determine state-wide primary results have not been fully accepted in the rules of the Wisconsin political game, and there is still no Democratic counterpart and hardly any analogous efforts at the local level by either party. That this situation is simply characteristic of still underdeveloped parties may not necessarily be true. It is also possible that a party in an environment like Wisconsin's, no matter how large its organized membership, would find it desirable to refrain from attempts to control the nominating process. This might result from an awareness of the difficulty of exerting control in an open primary state, but also from some sense of violating an established individualistic political credo.

That credo, it is suggested, appears to support a politics of personality that is at odds with a strict party responsibility doctrine. Instead of an elected official being held responsible to the voters through his party identification, there is the individualistic view, described in Chapter Two as part of Wisconsin's political culture, that the official is responsible directly and personally to the voters. The open primary method of nomination, when uncontrolled by a party organization, is a striking institutional manifestation of this outlook. So, too, is the direct election of a host of executive officers. Organizational influence, in this setting, becomes but one of several factors in determining results, though not to be dismissed as minor even in the Democratic party where activists are cultivated as collectively useful by aspiring candidates despite the ban on official organizational influence in the choice of nominees. Important, however, as party organizations may turn out to be, and they are surely worth closer study, an understanding of their role can hardly provide a complete picture of candidate selection or, more broadly, of political careers. What lies outside the framework of the responsible two-party model may be most enlightening with respect to the nature of the American political process, and in particular with respect to the characteristics which distinguish that process from European variants.

No very great beginning has been made in this work on the kind of study which would illuminate the nonparty characteristics of state politics. Some possibilities are suggested by the data of Chapter Six on the political careers of legislators, as well as by the material of Chapter Seven on the election of legislators. However, it seems useful to go well beyond these presentations, and to study intensively a number of individual politicians. This would involve a biographical approach, but one that would be explicitly focussed on such matters as the relation of candidacy for public office (or of party activism) to occupational status and aspiration, and the pattern of campaigning as affected by personal and interest-group considerations as well as by party organizations. The point is to try to comprehend as much as possible of the political process through the careers of individuals. Some of the substance of politics, which seems elusive when parties are the starting point for analysis, might thus be grasped.

NOTES AND SOURCES

NOTES

CHAPTER I

1 *American State Politics: An Introduction* (New York: Knopf, 1956).

2 Louis H. Bean, *Influences in the 1954 Mid-Term Elections* (Washington, D.C.: Public Affairs Institute, 1954), pp. 8–18. In the Republican landslide of 1952, McCarthy polled only 54 per cent of the vote compared to Eisenhower's 61 per cent (in Wisconsin), the incumbent Republican governor's 63 per cent, and even higher percentages for other Republican state office-holders.

CHAPTER II

1 U.S. Bureau of the Census, *U.S. Census of Population: 1950,* Vol. I, *Number of Inhabitants* (Washington, D.C.: U.S. Government Printing Office, 1952), Chap. 1, p. 14.

2 Douglas G. Marshall, *Wisconsin's Population—Changes and Prospects* (Madison: University of Wisconsin Agricultural Experiment Station, 1956), pp. 13–14.

3 Calculations are based on data contained in *U.S. Census of Population: 1950,* Vol. I, Chap. 49, "Wisconsin."

4 Data are derived from Table 2 of each appropriate chapter of Vol. I of *U.S. Census of Population: 1950.*

5 Marshall, *op. cit.,* pp. 15, 28.

6 *Wisconsin's Changing Population* (Madison: University of Wisconsin, 1942), p. 10.

7 Calculations, here and subsequently, of national origin are based on U.S. Bureau of the Census, *Fifteenth Census of the U.S.: 1930, Population,* Vol. III, Pt. 2, *Reports by States* (Washington, D.C.: U.S. Government Printing Office, 1932).

8 V. O. Key, Jr., *American State Politics: An Introduction* (New

York: Knopf, 1956), p. 243, happens to have tabulated data for Iowa, Kansas, Nebraska, Illinois, and New York on a number of subjects, including per cent foreign-born or of foreign-born or mixed parentage, and therefore these states are frequently used in the present chapter for comparison to Wisconsin.

9 Marshall, *op. cit.*, p. 13.
10 U.S. Bureau of the Census, *Religious Bodies: 1936* (Washington, D.C.: U.S. Government Printing Office, 1941), Vol. I, pp. 846–48.
11 Key, *op. cit.*, p. 244.
12 See *ibid.*, p. 239, for comparable data on other states.
13 *Statistical Abstract of the United States: 1953* (Washington, D.C.: U.S. Bureau of the Census, 1953), p. 291.
14 Marshall, *op. cit.*, pp. 31, 35, 37.
15 *Ibid.*, p. 56.
16 *Wisconsin Blue Book* (Madison: Wisconsin Legislative Reference Library, 1956), p. 559. Data originally from U.S. Bureau of Labor Statistics.
17 *Ibid.*, p. 566. Data originally from U.S. Bureau of the Census.
18 *Wis. Statutes,* Chap. 6 (1955), on elections.
19 *Ibid.*, Chap. 5 (1955), on nominations.
20 The entire story of Wisconsin's reapportionment battle is told by William H. Young, "Court Settles Apportionment," *National Municipal Review*, Vol. XLIII, pp. 398–402 (Sept., 1954). Some of the consequences will be analyzed in Chapter Seven.
21 Gordon E. Baker, *Rural Versus Urban Political Power* (Garden City, N.Y.: Doubleday, 1955), Chap. 3. However, it must be added that at least as yet Wisconsin's equitable representation in the state legislature has not produced a congressional redistricting in accord with the current distribution of population. The state's ten districts, shown on Figure 1, resemble the congressional pattern generally described by Baker. In particular, the districts of largely rural northern and northwestern Wisconsin have populations well below the norm, and the two Milwaukee districts have populations well above the norm.
22 Key, *op. cit.*, pp. 64–67.
23 *Wis. Statutes,* Chap. 12 (1955), on corrupt practices.

CHAPTER III

1 V. O. Key, Jr., *Southern Politics in State and Nation* (New York: Knopf, 1950), and Alexander Heard, *Two Party South?* (Chapel Hill: University of North Carolina Press, 1952).

2 Austin Ranney and Willmoore Kendall, "The American Party Systems," *American Political Science Review,* Vol. XLVIII, pp. 477–85 (June, 1954). Their "modified one-party" states include those in whose presidential, senatorial, and gubernatorial elections, from 1914 through 1952, the second party, while winning less than 25 per cent of all elections, nevertheless won over 30 per cent of the *vote* in over 70 per cent of all elections and won over 40 per cent of the *vote* in over 30 per cent of all elections. For a more involved system of classification, see Joseph A. Schlesinger, "A Two-Dimensional Scheme for Classifying the States According to Degree of Inter-party Competition," *American Political Science Review,* Vol. XLIX, pp. 1120–28 (Dec., 1955).

3 *Op. cit.,* p. 482. Added to the seven Democratic victories of the 1914–1952 period were six third-party victories (five by Progressives in state elections and one by the senior La Follette in the 1924 presidential race). Even the total of "second-party" wins reached by this procedure amounted to only 29.3 per cent of all 44 elections and so did not place Wisconsin very much above the minimum 25 per cent mark used by Ranney and Kendall to define their two-party states.

4 The state's presidential, gubernatorial, and senatorial election statistics are conveniently presented by James R. Donoghue, *How Wisconsin Voted 1848–1954* (Madison: University of Wisconsin Bureau of Government, 1956).

5 In 1873 the Democratic victory was related to the Granger movement and to a new law regulating saloons in a manner hostile to German-Americans. And in 1890 the Democratic success, maintained in 1892, was connected in part to a Republican law assumed to be hostile to the maintenance of parochial schools.—William F. Raney, *Wisconsin—A Story of Progress* (New York: Prentice-Hall, 1940), pp. 247, 251, 253, 267–68, 268.

6 The political composition of the state legislature during this period also reflected a two-party character, though of course usually with Republican majorities, as shown in the table pub-

lished by the Wisconsin Legislative Reference Library, *Wisconsin Blue Book* (Madison, 1954), p. 538.

7 Generalizations concerning early Wisconsin voting patterns rely heavily upon the careful and detailed studies of Joseph Schafer, particularly his "Who Elected Lincoln," *American Historical Review,* Vol. 47, pp. 51–63 (Oct., 1941); "The Yankee and the Teuton in Wisconsin," *Wisconsin Magazine of History,* Vol. VI, pp. 125–45, 260–79, 386–402 (1922–23), and Vol. VII, pp. 3–19, 148–71 (1923–24); *Four Wisconsin Counties* (Madison: State Historical Society, 1927); and *The Winnebago-Horicon Basin* (Madison: State Historical Society, 1937).

8 La Follette had come to believe during his earlier failures to obtain the Republican nomination that the convention system was conducive to political wrongdoing. Consequently, even though he certainly controlled the Republican convention by 1906, La Follette urged the substitution of the direct primary for nomination by convention. Ironically, in the first primary election (of 1906), the candidate La Follette himself supported for the gubernatorial nomination lost to another progressive.—Belle Case La Follette and Fola La Follette, *Robert M. La Follette* (New York: Macmillan, 1953), Vol. I, pp. 195, 213.

9 Key, *Southern Politics in State and Nation,* pp. 11–12, 16, 310.

10 The effect of these figures, when summarized, is to understate the frequency of multiple candidacies in the years of Republican dominance. The understatement results from the fact that included in the 1912–1946 period are the exceptionally lean Republican years of the mid-1930's when, temporarily, the Republican nomination was not attractive enough for much of a contest.

11 In 1922 the Republican primary vote was 104 per cent of the all-party general election vote, and in 1930 it was 109 per cent.

12 Compare the Wisconsin pattern, for example, to the consistently higher Democratic primary totals in southern states, as displayed in Table 13 of V. O. Key, Jr., *Politics, Parties and Pressure Groups* (New York: Thos. Y. Crowell, 1952), p. 427.

13 Because of the national Republican split in 1912, when La Follette was out of sympathy with both Taft and Roosevelt, that year is unusual in almost all respects. And in 1938 the Republican general election vote was inflated, compared with the party's primary vote, by the withdrawal of the Democratic

gubernatorial candidate so as to encourage conservative Democrats to vote Republican.

14 The volatility which these percentages indicate when compared with Wisconsin's heavy Republican presidential voting of the 1920's (Figure 3) has been said to characterize the states of the north-central and northwestern regions, and to be related to their progressive background.—Harold F. Gosnell and Morris H. Cohen, "Progressive Politics: Wisconsin an Example," *American Political Science Review,* Vol. XXXIV, pp. 920–35 (Oct., 1940).

15 Philip La Follette lost the governorship in 1932 by losing in the Republican primary to a stalwart, who subsequently was upset by a Democrat.

16 The history of La Follette's third party is carefully analyzed by Charles H. Backstrom, *The Progressive Party of Wisconsin, 1934–1946* (Unpublished Ph.D. dissertation, University of Wisconsin, 1956).

17 *Politics, Parties and Pressure Groups,* p. 316.

18 Indicative of the situation was the fact that when in 1948 Truman carried Wisconsin, the Democratic state ticket ran well behind, contrary to the tendency in many other states. Compare Illinois, for example.—*Ibid.,* pp. 308–9.

19 In the ninth district, the average per acre value of farm land and buildings is $60.72 (the mean of the averages in each of the 11 counties in the district), as compared with the state average of $88.58. Each of the 11 counties is more than 10 per cent below this state average, and all except one (which has continued to vote Republican) is more than 20 per cent below the state average.—*1950 U.S. Census of Agriculture,* Vol. I, Pt. 7 (Wisconsin), pp. 40–45.

20 Republicans lost the ninth district in 1953 after the incumbent Merlin Hull, an old-time Progressive, died. In a special election the seat was won for the first time by a Democrat (also a former Progressive), Lester Johnson, who was re-elected in 1954 and 1956.

21 Similar to the county-office pattern was the Republican dominance of the state legislature, described at length in Chapter Seven. Such continued dominance of the more local elections contrasted most sharply with the results of the special senatorial election of 1957, when the Democratic candidate carried 55 of the 71 counties and nine of the ten congressional districts.

22 In 26 of the 71 counties there were no candidates of either party for surveyor.

23 La Follette campaigned only briefly, in part because he underestimated (as did others after him) the prospects of McCarthy. Also the Senator was adversely affected by the particular efforts of the state CIO, then controlled by Communists, to keep its members from entering the Republican primary to vote for La Follette (just then a *bête noire* of the Communists because of his early postwar criticism of the Soviet Union).

24 In 1948, as in 1946, a La Follette follower named Ralph Immell failed to rally the old Progressive vote in his primary campaign against the regular Republican choice for governor. The decline from 1946 to 1948 is marked.

25 The voluntary organizations are analyzed in Chapter Five.

26 The type of correlation analysis employed here is quite properly open to objection if it is conceived as a substitute for individual correlation techniques—that is, for showing what proportion of former Progressive voters now vote Democratic. Counties, or any other geographical units, cannot give reliable results so far as individual behavior is concerned. This seems to me to have been conclusively demonstrated by W. S. Robinson, "Ecological Correlations and Behavior of Individuals," *American Sociological Review,* Vol. 15, pp. 351–57 (June, 1950). Therefore, all that is claimed for the present correlation analysis is that it shows some relation between *counties* which were Progressive and are now Democratic, and indicates that such counties probably have certain common characteristics.

27 Areas of Progressive strength are described in material prepared by the author for *How Wisconsin Voted 1848–1954,* pp. 24–27.

28 The coefficient of correlation was much lower (.25) when a different index of progressivism, based on 23 primary and general election contests from 1916 through 1946, was used with the 1948–1954 Democratic averages. Among other causes, the lower coefficient results from the fact that the earlier progressivism was more rurally oriented than that of the 1934–1946 period, and therefore even more so than the 1948–1954 Democratic strength.

29 *Op. cit.,* pp. 932–33.

30 These observations are derived from an analysis of Wisconsin's

twentieth-century vote according to the 13 economic areas into which the state is divided by the *1950 U.S. Census of Agriculture,* Vol. I, Pt. 7 (Wisconsin), p. 121. Only in the two areas mentioned (numbers 7 and 8 in Census terms) was there a pattern of higher-than-the-state-average Democratic percentages before 1934 and lower-than-the-state-average Democratic percentages in the 1948–1954 period.

31 An exception of a special sort was provided in 1957 by the seven-sided Republican primary to nominate a successor to Senator McCarthy. For this special election, no organizational endorsement was made. See Chapter Five.

32 For details on the McCarthy election of 1952, see Louis H. Bean, *Influences in the 1954 Mid-Term Elections* (Washington: Public Affairs Institute, 1954), Chap. iv; and also Samuel Lubell, *Revolt of the Moderates* (New York: Harper, 1956), for a discussion of German-American influences in McCarthy's election.

CHAPTER IV

1 In 1950, 1952, and 1954 the Republican candidate was Walter Kohler, and in 1948 Oscar Rennebohm. Both were businessmen and considered relatively good vote-getters. The Democratic candidates were Carl Thompson in 1948 and 1950, and William Proxmire in 1952 and 1954. Neither Democrat had achieved prominence outside of partisan political activities, but both were counted as vigorous campaigners. In particular, Proxmire was so steadily vigorous that by 1956, when he ran a third time for governor, he had achieved an unusual status. The same must be said, of course, for Proxmire's successful race in 1957 for the U.S. Senate seat left vacant by McCarthy's death. See pp. 72–75 of this chapter.

2 For example, note the survey data of Elmo Roper and Louis Harris, published in "Crime, Reform and the Voter," *Saturday Review of Literature,* Vol. 34, pp. 7–9, 34–35 (April 7, 1951). Also note the reference in V. O. Key, Jr., *Politics, Parties and Pressure Groups* (New York: Thos. Y. Crowell, 1952), p. 272.

3 A very broad working-class grouping, useful for his purposes but not apparently for mine, is made by Duncan MacRae, Jr., in his excellent study of "Occupations and the Congressional Vote," *American Sociological Review,* Vol. 20, pp. 332–40 (June, 1955). He defines the "labor vote" as including all

craftsmen, operatives, and nonfarm laborers. But, as noted later in my study, MacRae finds that the decrease in this labor vote, like the decrease in manufacturing employment, is not sufficient to account for the drop in the Democratic percentage from more urban to less urban areas.

4   Excellent use of different Census occupational data has been made in a study of Milwaukee voting by Andrew R. Baggaley, "White Collar Employment and Republican Vote," *Public Opinion Quarterly,* Vol. XX, pp. 471–73 (Summer, 1956).

5   U.S. Bureau of the Census, *U.S. Census of Population: 1950,* Vol. II, *Characteristics of Population,* Part 49, Wisconsin, Chapter B (Washington, D.C.: U.S. Government Printing Office, 1952), Tables 10 and 11.

6   *Ibid.,* Table 34. By 1950, of course, foreign-born percentages were generally low.

7   "Two general social factors that correlate with leftist voting are size of individual plants and size of cities."—S. M. Lipset, P. J. Lazarsfeld, A. H. Barton, and J. Linz, "The Psychology of Voting: An Analysis of Political Behavior," *Handbook of Social Psychology,* Vol. II, p. 1141, ed. by G. Lindzey (Cambridge, Mass.: Addison-Wesley, 1954).

8   The same general phenomenon was observed in the 1930's by Harold F. Gosnell and Morris H. Cohen, "Progressive Politics: Wisconsin an Example," *American Political Science Review,* Vol. XXXIV, p. 928 (Oct., 1940).

9   *U.S. Census of Population: 1950,* Vol. II, *Characteristics of Population,* Pt. 49.

10 Lipset, Lazarsfeld, Barton, and Linz, *op. cit.,* p. 1166.

11 V. O. Key, Jr., *American State Politics* (New York: Knopf, 1956), p. 227.

12 Bernard R. Berelson, Paul F. Lazarsfeld, and William N. McPhee, *Voting* (Chicago: University of Chicago Press, 1954), p. 57.

13 Joseph Rosenstein, "Party Politics: Unequal Contest," in W. Lloyd Warner, *Democracy in Jonesville* (New York: Harper, 1949), p. 217.

14 MacRae, *op. cit.,* p. 334. See my note 3 for MacRae's definition of "non-farm labor occupations."

15 General corroboration of this finding with respect to the farm vote is provided by the *Wisconsin Agriculturalist and Farmer* (Jan. 1, 1955, p. 18), which found that the Democratic candidate in 1954 won 52 per cent of the vote in those townships

in which 80 per cent or more of the adults were farm people. This compared to a mere 29.7 per cent polled in the same townships by the Democrat in 1952.

16 Fairly elaborate attempts to relate the farm vote to economic wealth, ethnic background, and farm organizational membership were made in my study, *The Wisconsin Farm Vote for Governor, 1948–1954* (Madison: University of Wisconsin Bureau of Government, 1956).

17 Gosnell and Cohen, *op. cit.*

18 For example, in the national survey of behavior in the presidential elections of 1948 and 1952 by Angus Campbell, Gerald Gurin, and Warren E. Miller, *The Voter Decides* (Evanston: Row, Peterson & Co., 1954), a particularly pronounced swing in the vote of "rural areas" is observed in relation to the vote in two other types of community, "metropolitan areas" and "towns and cities" (pp. 71, 74).

19 This omits the 1956 election because the returns for that year have not been tabulated according to size of place. However, it is plain from an examination of the presidential returns that the farm revolt was recorded at least moderately against even Eisenhower's personal popularity. The President's percentage of the two-party vote dropped from 1952 to 1956 in 45 counties, mainly rural, while his state-wide percentage increased slightly thanks to larger urban majorities in 1956 than in 1952.

CHAPTER V

1 Maurice Duverger, *Political Parties,* trans. by Barbara and Robert North (London: Methuen, 1954), pp. 5, 23, 427. For a discussion of highly developed mass-membership organizations, see R. T. McKenzie, *British Political Parties* (London: Heinemann, 1955). The same phenomena are discussed in a different perspective in the present author's "British Mass Parties in Comparison with American Parties," *Political Science Quarterly,* Vol. LXXXI, pp. 97–125 (March, 1956).

2 Similar organizations in California are briefly described by Currin Shields, "A Note on Party Organization: The Democrats in California," *Western Political Quarterly,* Vol. VII, pp. 673–84 (Dec., 1954); and by Hugh Bone, "New Party Associations in the West," *American Political Science Review,* Vol. XLV, pp. 1115–25 (Dec., 1951). Among others, the Michigan parties are also similar, and in the past there have

been dues-paying third parties, socialist and farmer-labor, in the United States.

3 Distinguishable from this usual type, though in a different way from the Wisconsin parties, is the substantial old-style organization described so thoroughly by Roy V. Peel, *The Political Clubs of New York City* (New York: Putnam's, 1935).

4 Customarily few committed partisans actually engage in campaign work, and in a recent Detroit study it was found that fewer than 20 per cent of even the hard core of each party's voters were thus engaged.—Samuel J. Eldersveld, *Political Affiliation in Metropolitan Detroit* (Ann Arbor: University of Michigan Bureau of Government, 1957), p. 157.

5 Frank J. Sorauf, "Extra-Legal Political Parties in Wisconsin," *American Political Science Review,* Vol. XLVIII, pp. 692–704 (Sept., 1954).

6 "Middle-class" is used in the loose and usual sense to mean that part of the urban community which is distinguished from the manual working class by occupation and residential housing values.

7 Based on reports filed with the secretary of state, these estimates probably understate actual expenditures.

8 Following the 1954 election, when the state Democratic campaign appeared to be financed for the first time on a scale similar to that of the Republicans, the Republican state legislature enacted the "Catlin law," designed, as already pointed out in Chapter Two, to parallel in state politics the Taft-Hartley ban on union contributions nationally. So far, however, the main effect of the state ban has been for unions to substitute "political education" among their members for their former direct financial contributions to Democratic campaign committees.

9 Generally these figures are not impressively high by British standards. For example, while the Democrats have enrolled about one in every 350 Wisconsin residents, the British Conservatives have about one of every 50 Englishmen.

10 A leading example, encountered in the course of field study, is provided by the large and highly effective Republican organization in what is historically the state's most Republican county, where no offices at the county level are seriously contested by Democrats and where the Republican presidential and gubernatorial percentages stand at about 70 per cent. Naturally Republican activists feel that their national and state candidates

will benefit by a turnout when 7 out of 10 voters are likely to vote Republican. Interestingly there is also an active though less numerous Democratic club in this country, and it is devoted to the still utopian goal of raising to 40 per cent the county vote polled by its state-wide candidates.

11 Although there are only 338 questionnaires, the total number of answers here is 407 because of a double count of those questionnaires on which two of the three choices (national, state, and local) were checked. (When all three were checked, the questionnaires are counted as indefinite.)

12 Eldersveld, *op. cit.*, p. 127.

13 *Milwaukee Journal,* June 26, 1955.

14 *Ibid.*, May 27, 1956.

15 *Ibid.*, June 9, 1957.

16 That fewer years of party membership and party service mean that Democrats are also younger than Republicans is indicated but not established. Only for the Milwaukee unit officers were data obtained on age. These data did show that the Democratic officers were about as many years younger in age as in party membership and activity.

17 "One-party Republican," in this connection, refers to any county in which the Republican vote for governor was 55 per cent or more in the peak Democratic year of 1954 and in which all legislators elected in 1954 and 1956 by voters of the given county were Republicans.

18 For example, in Eldersveld's Detroit study of even the hard core of partisan followers, almost three-fifths of the Republican followers but only 3 per cent of the Democrats came from professional and business-managerial classes (p. 158).

19 In many of Wisconsin's villages and cities below about 20,000 population, the Democrats lack leaders for the reasons given by Key in his discussion of northern states in general: "Well-connected lawyers, businessmen with time and money to devote to politics, and, perhaps to a lesser extent, persons with skill in professional politics gravitate in greater degree to the Republican party than to the Democratic."—V. O. Key, Jr., *American State Politics* (New York: Knopf, 1956), p. 257.

20 The Milwaukee ward units are in this instance too few to support the calculation of percentages.

21 Harold F. Gosnell, *Machine Politics: Chicago Model* (Chicago: University of Chicago Press, 1937), pp. 40–41.

22 *Op. cit.*, p. 127.

23 *Milwaukee Journal,* June 9, 1957.
24 George Smith originally secured office as a result of winning a five-cornered Republican primary in 1948, when there was no party endorsement. He was never viewed as a regular.
25 *Milwaukee Journal,* May 27, 1956. This newspaper, in a three-column front-page photograph of a "lonely" Senator Wiley leaving the convention hall, helped to set the stage for the Senator's subsequently successful appeal to the primary electorate against the decision of the "machine."
26 *Ibid.,* June 9, 1957.
27 The proposal, framed in mid-1957 for submission to the Democratic convention in the fall of that year, would have required endorsement for state-wide offices except where a convention by two-thirds vote rejected such action, and would have permitted congressional, legislative, and county units to endorse provided a minimum membership standard was met. The latter, it is worth noting, was supported by Milwaukee politicians, including some labor leaders, who are most concerned to control the bestowal of the party label locally, since in most parts of Milwaukee Democratic primary nomination virtually ensures election.
28 The Madison *Capital Times,* once the voice of La Follette progressivism and now pro-Democratic, has editorialized that the Democrats "should be the last people to advocate a practice which is aimed at gutting the open primary law, which was made law in this state by the untiring efforts of Old Bob La Follette" (August 10, 1955).
29 The Democratic politician who was the principal opponent of endorsement, William Proxmire, had his individualistic principles fortified by his demonstrated capacity to win the Democratic primary—three times for governor and once for U.S. senator—and finally by his election to the Senate in 1957. He struck a blow against what many Democrats considered his own cause in 1956 when, while running for governor in the general election, he decided to repudiate as unqualified his party's successful primary candidate for attorney general and to foster an Independent Democratic candidate instead. However, such personal endorsement (or disendorsement) may be less offensive to Wisconsin's individualistic tradition than organizational action. The father of this tradition, the elder La Follette, had regularly given his personal blessing to a primary candidate of his own choosing at the same time that he de-

nounced similar action by conventions. To communicate his endorsement to his followers, La Follette used his own magazine as well as usual political channels.

CHAPTER VI

1   Salary data on legislators in other states are found in *American Legislatures: Structure and Procedures* (Chicago: Council of State Governments, 1955), pp. 6–11 and Table 3.

2   The distinction between professional and part-time legislative service does not coincide with Max Weber's distinction between those who "live 'off' politics as a vocation" and those who live " 'for' politics." One may regard politics as his vocation but still consider legislative service as a part-time incident in the long-run pursuit of that vocation. See *From Max Weber: Essays in Sociology*, ed. and trans. by H. H. Gerth and C. W. Mills (New York: Oxford University Press, 1946), p. 84.

3   *American Legislatures: Structure and Procedures.*

4   *Milwaukee Journal,* Feb. 10, 1957, p. 1.

5   Charles S. Hyneman, "Tenure and Turnover of Legislative Personnel," *The Annals of the American Academy of Political and Social Science,* Vol. 195, pp. 21–31 (1938).

6   *Ibid.,* p. 30.

7   The significance of age in relation to legislative attitudes is one of several items explored by John B. McConaughy, "Certain Personality Factors of State Legislators in South Carolina," *American Political Science Review,* Vol. XLIV, pp. 897–903 (Dec., 1950).

8   Wisconsin Legislative Reference Library, *Wisconsin Blue Book* (Madison, 1956), p. 602.

9   Belle Zeller, *American State Legislatures* (New York: Crowell, 1954), p. 70.

10   Wisconsin Legislative Reference Library, *The Profile of a Legislature* (Madison, 1956), p. 14.

11   V. O. Key, Jr., *American State Politics* (New York: Knopf, 1956), pp. 259–60.

12   As has been said of lawyers (Weber, *op. cit.,* p. 85), real estate and insurance men also seem relatively dispensable, in an economic sense, from their occupations.

13   Mobility in a different sense was explored by asking legislators whether their fathers had been in politics, either as public officeholders, candidates, or party officers. Returns from 111

legislators showed that three-fourths of their fathers had not been in politics, thus defined.

14 Edward A. Shils, "The Legislator and His Environment," *University of Chicago Law Review,* Vol. 18, pp. 571–84 (Spring, 1951), at p. 581.

15 "Higher" occupational status is admittedly an inexact term, since it usually includes both the professions, which do require more formal education, and entrepreneurial positions, which do not always require more formal education than other occupations. However, the usage here obviates this difficulty since, as it happens, concern is with movement from other occupations into the professions. For a general discussion of the subject, see William H. Form and Delbert C. Miller, "Occupational Career Pattern as a Sociological Instrument," *American Journal of Sociology,* Vol. LIV, pp. 317–29 (Jan., 1949).

16 James Willard Hurst, *The Growth of American Law* (Boston: Little, Brown, 1950), p. 254.

17 An interesting sidelight is provided by the presence in most Wisconsin legislative sessions of a few University law *students* getting a running start in their politico-legal careers and also happily adding legislative salaries to their student incomes while in Madison. Obviously, these student-legislators cannot be serious legal scholars during legislative sessions or during campaigning seasons.

18 Maurice Liebenberg, *Income of Lawyers in the Postwar Period* (Washington, D.C.: U.S. Department of Commerce [reprint from *Survey of Current Business*], Dec., 1956), p. 2.

19 *Ibid.,* p. 11.

20 As Duncan MacRae, Jr., has pointed out, the situation of a state representative, in pleasing his constituents, is more like that of an entrepreneur or a professional seeking a clientele than it is like that of a salaried employee, and so it is possible that political entry of those engaged in independent occupations may be explained by "selective factors in temperament" similar to those required of entrepreneurs or independent professionals.—"The Role of the State Legislator in Massachusetts," *American Sociological Review,* Vol. 19, pp. 185–94 (April, 1954), at p. 188.

21 Weber, *op. cit.,* p. 94.

22 Hurst, *op. cit.,* pp. 49, 352.

23 For a contrast between political and bureaucratic careers, see

Everett C. Hughes, "Institutional Office and the Person," *American Journal of Sociology,* Vol. XLIII, pp. 404–13 (Nov., 1937), at p. 413. This and certain other references on the subject of careers were first called to my attention in a memorandum by Professor Lester Seligman, a collaborator in the political recruitment study sponsored by the Social Science Research Council.

24 With respect to state constitutional offices, the percentage of legislators elected is lower for this 1925–1955 period than it was over most of Wisconsin's history up to 1937, as shown by John Brown Mason, "The State Legislature as Training for Future Public Service," *The Annals of the American Academy of Political and Social Science,* Vol. 195, pp. 176–82 (1938), at p. 176. Other routes to higher state offices, probably nongovernmental office routes, have evidently assumed greater relative importance in recent years.

25 An analysis of the special relation of law to political advancement, really of the combination of law with a long-range political career leading to the governorship, is made by Joseph A. Schlesinger, "Lawyers and American Politics: A Clarified View," *Midwest Journal of Political Science,* Vol. I, pp. 26–39 (May, 1957). Also Schlesinger has shown that state legislatures have become less important as a source for governors since 1870. See *How They Became Governor* (East Lansing: Michigan State University Government Research Bureau, 1957), p. 51.

26 Candidacies should not be expressed as a percentage of the number of election contests because these contests often included several losing candidates, in the primary or even in the general election during the state's three-party period, 1934–1944.

27 *Wis. Statutes,* 13.62–68 (1955).

28 Wis. Laws 1947, c. 609.

29 Based on an examination of records of the Wisconsin secretary of state.

30 Madison *Capital Times,* July 15, 1957, p. 28.

31 Some findings on similar matters in another state were reported by Paul Beckett and Celeste Sunderland, "Washington State's Lawmakers: Some Personal Factors in the Washington Legislature," *Western Political Quarterly,* Vol. X, pp. 180–202 (March, 1957).

CHAPTER VII

1 Gordon E. Baker, *Rural Versus Urban Political Power* (Garden City, N.Y.: Doubleday, 1955), p. 17.
2 Wisconsin Legislative Council—Legislative Reapportionment Committee, *Report on Reapportionment* (Madison: State of Wisconsin, 1951), Chap. 2.
3 V. O. Key, Jr., *American State Politics* (New York: Knopf, 1956), p. 64.
4 *Ibid.,* pp. 27, 208.
5 See Table II-A. Counted among the 63 pro-daylight-saving districts is a three-county constituency in which one county voted against daylight saving.
6 During this period, one other seat changed hands, passing to the Democrats in 1954 and back to the Republicans in 1956, but it does not appear to have been decisively affected by reapportionment.
7 Before 1932 Socialists had been numerous among Milwaukee legislators.
8 Leadership positions have been dominated by rural Republicans. Of the committee chairmanships, 26 of 32 in 1955 and 29 of 38 in 1957 were held by legislators from districts classified as rural.
9 *Milwaukee Journal,* June 30, 1957, sect. 1, p. 18.
10 This finding contrasts with Charles S. Hyneman's for eight state legislatures in the period 1925–1935.—"Tenure and Turnover of Legislative Personnel," *The Annals of the American Academy of Political and Social Science,* Vol. 195, pp. 21–31 (1938), at p. 26. He found only about the same percentage (15.6 per cent) defeated in primaries as in general elections (15.9 per cent). This suggests that the primary has been relatively more important in Wisconsin than elsewhere, and this suggestion is referred to again later in the discussion.
11 "Primary Elections as the Alternative to Party Competition in Safe Districts," *Journal of Politics,* Vol. 15, pp. 197–210 (May, 1953). See also the general discussion in Chapter Three of primary competition for state-wide offices in Wisconsin.
12 Key, *op. cit.,* Chap. 6.
13 *Ibid.,* p. 174.
14 *Ibid.,* pp. 172–75.
15 *Ibid.,* p. 179.

16 *Ibid.,* p. 177.
17 Turner, *op. cit.,* p. 203.
18 Key, *op. cit.,* pp. 181–82, 190, 194.
19 *Ibid.,* p. 196.
20 These data are available because of candidate biographies collected and published by the *Milwaukee Journal* (in special sections on Sept. 7, 1956, and Nov. 2, 1956). The methods by which this newspaper compiles its biographies should be the envy of political scientists. Candidates are simply summoned to the *Journal* office for an interview, and if they refuse to appear or to answer reporters' questions the *Journal* obligingly informs its readers of the refusal. Candidates are inclined to be coöperative.
21 "Strong-Republican" and "strong-Democratic" are used here to mean a district in which the last legislative general election was won with 55 per cent or more of the vote.
22 In 1956 the Republicans did have a legislative election committee designed to help win marginal seats.
23 For general discussion of parties in state legislatures, see Belle Zeller, *American State Legislatures* (New York: Crowell, 1954), pp. 192–94, and William J. Keefe, "Comparative Study of the Role of Political Parties in State Legislatures," *Western Political Quarterly,* Vol. 9, pp. 726–42 (Sept., 1956).
24 *Wis. Statutes,* 12.20 (1955).
25 Key, *op. cit.,* p. 169.

CHAPTER VIII

1 E. E. Schattschneider, "United States: The Functional Approach to Party Government," in *Modern Political Parties,* ed. by Sigmund Neumann (Chicago: University of Chicago Press, 1956), p. 209.
2 Heinz Eulau has found that competitive party systems are more likely in metropolitan and urban situations than in counties which are small-town or rural in character.—"The Ecological Basis of Party Systems: The Case of Ohio," *Midwest Journal of Political Science,* Vol. I, pp. 125–35 (August, 1957). His findings are persuasive, but they seem to relate to competition in whole counties rather than in districts within counties. Understood in this way, the case of Ohio is similar to that of Wisconsin, where, as shown earlier, it is in metropolitan and urban counties that both major parties are organized with some effectiveness.

APPENDIX

TABLE II-A
DAYLIGHT-SAVING TIME REFERENDUM—1957

County	Total Vote	For Vote	For Per Cent	Against Vote	Against Per Cent
Adams	2,462	664	27.0	1,798	73.0
Ashland	6,682	3,059	45.8	3,623	54.2
Barron	9,658	2,966	30.7	6,692	69.3
Bayfield	3,470	1,300	37.5	2,170	62.5
Brown	38,891	24,490	63.0	14,401	37.0
Buffalo	3,698	684	18.5	3,014	81.5
Burnett	2,872	801	27.9	2,071	72.1
Calumet	5,849	2,329	39.8	3,520	60.2
Chippewa	12,303	4,619	37.5	7,684	62.5
Clark	8,993	2,251	25.0	6,742	75.0
Columbia	10,417	3,935	37.8	6,482	62.2
Crawford	4,718	818	17.3	3,900	82.7
Dane	55,185	31,644	57.3	23,541	42.7
Dodge	17,688	7,591	42.9	10,097	57.1
Door	6,367	2,762	43.4	3,605	56.6
Douglas	14,221	5,955	41.9	8,266	58.1
Dunn	6,851	1,558	22.7	5,293	77.3
Eau Claire	13,184	6,667	50.6	6,517	49.4
Florence	1,217	486	39.9	731	60.1
Fond du Lac	22,134	11,155	50.4	10,979	49.6
Forest	3,140	1,446	46.1	1,694	53.9
Grant	11,619	2,191	18.9	9,428	81.1
Green	7,649	1,780	23.3	5,869	76.7
Green Lake	5,893	2,388	40.5	3,505	59.5
Iowa	6,706	1,252	18.7	5,454	81.3
Iron	2,386	1,122	47.0	1,264	53.0
Jackson	4,320	1,044	24.2	3,276	75.8
Jefferson	15,626	7,191	46.0	8,435	54.0
Juneau	5,475	1,631	29.8	3,844	70.2
Kenosha	29,996	19,710	65.7	10,286	34.3
Kewaunee	6,001	2,207	36.8	3,794	63.2
La Crosse	21,299	10,901	51.2	10,398	48.8
Lafayette	5,898	955	16.2	4,943	83.8
Langlade	6,380	2,441	38.3	3,939	61.7
Lincoln	6,511	3,269	50.2	3,242	49.8

TABLE II - A (Cont.)

County	Total Vote	For Vote	For Per Cent	Against Vote	Against Per Cent
Manitowoc	22,056	13,641	61.8	8,415	38.2
Marathon	25,057	12,197	48.7	12,860	51.3
Marinette	10,216	4,751	46.5	5,465	53.5
Marquette	2,949	660	22.4	2,289	77.6
Milwaukee	242,987	184,599	76.0	58,388	24.0
Monroe	9,094	2,779	30.6	6,315	69.4
Oconto	7,849	2,909	37.1	4,940	62.9
Oneida	7,147	4,244	59.4	2,903	40.6
Outagamie	26,340	15,844	60.2	10,496	39.8
Ozaukee	10,528	6,983	66.3	3,545	33.7
Pepin	1,741	427	24.5	1,314	75.5
Pierce	5,970	1,292	21.6	4,678	78.4
Polk	6,298	1,607	25.5	4,691	74.5
Portage	12,130	6,304	52.0	5,826	48.0
Price	4,933	1,953	39.6	2,980	60.4
Racine	36,267	23,139	63.8	13,128	36.2
Richland	5,812	831	14.3	4,981	85.7
Rock	24,501	13,065	53.3	11,436	46.7
Rusk	3,804	1,077	28.3	2,727	71.7
St. Croix	7,707	2,048	26.6	5,659	73.4
Sauk	10,156	3,366	33.1	6,790	66.9
Sawyer	3,215	1,112	34.6	2,103	65.4
Shawano	9,110	3,410	37.4	5,700	62.6
Sheboygan	27,773	15,246	54.9	12,527	45.1
Taylor	4,900	1,519	31.0	3,381	69.0
Trempealeau	6,485	1,473	22.7	5,012	77.3
Vernon	8,186	1,249	15.3	6,937	84.7
Vilas	3,909	2,271	58.1	1,638	41.9
Walworth	14,499	7,937	54.7	6,562	45.3
Washburn	3,029	869	28.7	2,160	71.3
Washington	11,859	6,147	51.8	5,712	48.2
Waukesha	37,430	26,663	71.2	10,767	28.8
Waupaca	10,647	4,270	40.1	6,377	59.9
Waushara	4,291	1,089	25.4	3,202	74.6
Winnebago	28,959	18,782	64.9	10,177	35.1
Wood	15,724	7,646	48.6	8,078	51.4
State	1,059,317	578,661	54.6	480,656	45.4

TABLE III-A

REPUBLICAN PRIMARY CANDIDATES, 1912–1956

Year	Gubernatorial			Senatorial		
	Total No.	No. over 5% of Vote	Majority or Plurality	Total No.	No. over 5% of Vote	Majority or Plurality
1912	1	1	M			
1914	6	6	P	6	6	P
1916	4	3	P	2	2	M
1918	3	3	P			
1920	6	6	P	3	3	P
1922	3	2	M	2	2	M
1924	3	3	M			
1926	4	4	P	3	3	M
1928	4	3	P	2	2	M
1930	2	2	M			
1932	2	2	M	2	2	M
1934	3	3	M	1	1	M
1936	2	2	M			
1938	4	3	M	6	6	P
1940	2	2	M	7	7	P
1942	3	3	M			
1944	5	4	P	4	3	M
1946	5	3	P	3	3	P
1948	2	2	M			
1950	2	2	M	2	2	M
1952	1	1	M	6	2	M
1954	1	1	M			
1956	1	1	M	3	2	P

TABLE III-B
TWO-PARTY PERCENTAGES OF GUBERNATORIAL AND
CONGRESSIONAL VOTE, 1948–1956

Year	Congressional Vote		Gubernatorial Vote	
	Rep.	Dem.	Rep.	Dem.
State-wide (10 Congressional Districts)				
1948	56.8	43.2	55.1	44.9
1950	57.6	42.4	53.6	46.4
1952	61.6	38.4	62.6	37.4
1954	52.5	47.5	51.5	48.5
1956	54.2	45.8	51.9	48.1
Milwaukee County (2 Congressional Districts)				
1948	43.7	56.3	46.9	53.1
1950	45.6	54.4	45.9	54.1
1952	43.9	56.1	48.9	51.1
1954	38.6	61.4	44.3	55.7
1956	38.4	61.6	44.0	56.0
Outside Milwaukee County (8 Congressional Districts)				
1948	61.7	38.3	58.0	42.0
1950	61.8	38.2	56.2	43.8
1952	68.1	31.9	67.6	32.4
1954	57.2	42.8	54.0	46.0
1956	59.9	40.1	54.7	45.3

TABLE III-C
TWO-PARTY PERCENTAGES OF TOTAL VOTE CAST
FOR COUNTY SHERIFFS, DISTRICT ATTORNEYS,
AND GOVERNOR, 1954

	Sheriff		Dist. Atty.		Governor	
	Rep.	Dem.	Rep.	Dem.	Rep.	Dem.
State-Wide	55.6	44.4	60.2	39.8	51.5	48.5
Milwaukee County Only	39.7	60.3	32.8	67.2	44.3	55.7
Outside Milwaukee County	61.4	38.6	71.0	29.0	54.0	46.0

TABLE V-A

PARTY OFFICERS WHO HAVE BEEN DELEGATES OR ALTERNATES
AT PARTY CONVENTIONS (Per Cent)

Delegate or alternate	Republican officers					Democratic officers				Total: Rep. & Dem.
	County chairmen	County secs.	Women's leaders	Milw. officers	Total	County chairmen	County secs.	Milw. officers	Total	
State conventions										
Yes	100.0	94.8	87.2	100.0	95.6	95.3	89.2	69.2	88.4	92.3
No	0.0	5.2	12.8	0.0	4.4	4.7	10.8	30.8	11.6	7.7
Indefinite	0.0	0.0	0.0	0.0	0.0	0.0	0.0	0.0	0.0	0.0
Total	100.0	100.0	100.0	100.0	100.0	100.0	100.0	100.0	100.0	100.0
National conventions										
Yes	21.9	1.7	33.3	4.5	15.8	20.3	12.3	15.4	16.1	16.0
No	76.6	98.3	64.1	90.9	82.5	78.1	87.7	84.6	83.2	82.8
Indefinite	1.6	0.0	2.6	4.5	1.6	1.6	0.0	0.0	0.6	1.2
Total	100.1	100.0	100.0	99.9	99.9	100.0	100.0	100.0	99.9	100.0
Number	64	58	39	22	183	64	65	26	155	338

TABLE V-B
OCCUPATIONS OF PARTY OFFICERS
(Per Cent)

Occupation	Republican officers					Democratic officers				Total: Rep. & Dem.
	County chairmen	County secs.	Women's leaders	Milw. officers	Total	County chairmen	County secs.	Milw. officers	Total	
Lawyer	29.7	19.0	0.0	18.2	18.6	18.8	9.2	19.2	14.8	16.9
Teacher	3.1	5.2	5.1	4.5	4.4	4.7	4.6	3.8	4.5	4.4
Other profession	9.4	10.3	7.7	9.1	9.3	1.6	0.0	3.8	1.3	5.6
Business-managerial	45.3	19.0	5.1	22.7	25.7	17.2	12.3	3.8	12.9	19.8
Farmer	3.1	3.4	0.0	0.0	2.2	15.6	7.7	0.0	9.7	5.6
Sales-clerical	4.7	6.9	10.3	36.4	10.4	7.8	16.9	26.9	14.8	12.4
Manual worker	0.0	3.4	0.0	9.1	2.2	23.4	16.9	26.9	21.3	10.9
Local gov't. official	0.0	13.8	0.0	0.0	4.4	1.6	3.1	3.8	2.6	3.6
Retired	3.1	1.7	2.6	0.0	2.2	3.1	4.6	0.0	3.2	2.7
Housewife	0.0	17.2	69.2	0.0	20.2	4.7	23.1	11.5	13.5	17.2
Indefinite	1.6	0.0	0.0	0.0	0.5	1.6	1.5	0.0	1.3	0.9
Total	100.0	99.9	100.0	100.0	100.1	100.1	99.9	99.7	99.9	100.0
Number	64	58	39	22	183	64	65	26	155	338

TABLE V-C

CANDIDACY OF PARTY OFFICERS FOR ELECTIVE PUBLIC OFFICES

(Per Cent)

Elective public office	Republican officers					Democratic officers				Total: Rep. & Dem.
	County chairmen	County secs.	Women's leaders	Milw. officers	Total	County chairmen	County secs.	Milw. officers	Total	
Elected to:										
Yes	51.6	44.8	12.8	22.7	37.7	39.1	24.6	15.4	29.0	33.7
No	48.4	55.2	84.6	77.3	61.7	59.4	75.4	84.6	70.3	65.7
Indefinite	0.0	0.0	2.6	0.0	0.5	1.6	0.0	0.0	0.6	0.6
Total	100.0	100.0	100.0	100.0	99.9	100.1	100.0	100.0	99.9	100.0
Defeated for:										
Yes	39.1	13.8	5.1	59.1	26.2	54.7	36.9	34.6	43.9	34.3
No	60.9	84.5	87.2	40.9	71.6	42.2	60.0	65.4	53.5	63.3
Indefinite	0.0	1.7	7.7	0.0	2.2	3.1	3.1	0.0	2.6	2.4
Total	100.0	100.0	100.0	100.0	100.0	100.0	100.0	100.0	100.0	100.0
Intend to run for:										
Yes	15.6	24.1	5.1	22.7	16.9	34.4	12.3	38.5	25.8	21.0
No	76.6	69.0	87.2	68.2	75.4	53.1	78.5	57.7	64.5	70.4
Indefinite	7.8	6.9	7.7	9.1	7.7	12.5	9.2	3.8	9.7	8.6
Total	100.0	100.0	100.0	100.0	100.0	100.0	100.0	100.0	100.0	100.0
Desire to run for:										
Yes	23.4	29.3	15.4	50.0	26.8	48.4	36.9	57.7	45.2	35.2
No	67.2	60.3	76.9	40.9	63.9	42.2	58.5	42.3	49.0	57.1
Indefinite	9.4	10.3	7.7	9.1	9.3	9.4	4.6	0.0	5.8	7.7
Total	100.0	99.9	100.0	100.0	100.0	100.0	100.0	100.0	100.0	100.0
Number	64	58	39	22	183	64	65	26	155	338

TABLE VI-A
COMPARISON OF LEGISLATORS WHO ANSWERED
QUESTIONNAIRES WITH THE FULL LEGISLATIVE
MEMBERSHIP (1957)

Characteristic	All Members	Responding Members
Number	133	111
Median age	49.0	50.5
Legislative house (per cent)		
Senate	24.8	23.4
Assembly	75.2	76.6
Total	100.0	100.0
Party (per cent)		
Republican	67.7	68.5
Democrat	32.3	31.5
Total	100.0	100.0
Urban-rural status* (per cent)		
Urban	45.9	45.0
Rural	54.1	55.0
Total	100.0	100.0
Party competition † (per cent)		
Strong-Republican	50.4	51.4
Strong-Democratic	25.6	26.1
Two-party competitive	24.1	22.5
Total	100.1	100.0
Education (per cent)		
Less than high school	17.3	18.0
High school	19.5	18.9
Some college (no degree)	14.3	10.8
College degree	15.8	16.2
Advanced degree	32.3	35.1
Indefinite	0.8	0.9
Total	100.0	99.9
Legislative service (per cent)		
First term	31.6	35.1
Second term	25.6	25.2
Third term	14.3	13.5
Fourth term	8.3	5.4
Fifth term	8.3	9.0
Sixth term or more	12.0	11.7
Total	100.1	99.9
Occupation ‡ (per cent)		
Attorney	30.1	33.3
Other profession	3.8	4.5
Business-managerial	17.3	18.9
Farmer	18.0	21.6
Sales-clerical	11.3	9.0
Manual worker	7.5	8.1
Local government official	0.8	0.9
Retired	4.5	0.9
Indefinite	6.8	2.7
Total	100.1	99.9

TABLE VI-B
LEGISLATIVE SERVICE

Assemblymen (100)

Legislative session	Ex-Senators	Assembly terms													
		1	2	3	4	5	6	7	8	9	10	11	12	13	14
1951	1	29	27	13	7	9	3	4	3	2	2	1	0	0	0
1953	1	22	24	22	8	5	7	4	1	3	2	1	1	0	0
1955	0	36	17	13	15	4	2	5	1	2	2	2	0	1	0
1957	1	29	26	13	8	9	4	0	4	1	2	1	2	0	1

Senators (33)

Legislative session	Ex-Assemblymen	Senate terms						
		1	2	3	4	5	6	7
1951	9	12	9	7	4	0	1	0
1953	10	10	11	5	5	1	0	1
1955	14	16	9	2	2	4	0	0
1957	13	16	9	3	1	1	3	0

NOTES TO TABLE VI - A (facing page)

*"Urban" here means those districts in which over half of the population lives in cities over 10,000 or in Census-classified urbanized areas, and "rural" includes all remaining districts. As explained in the text, it is this definition which is generally used in tabulations in this chapter and the next. Unless otherwise indicated, "urban" and "rural" may be so understood whenever noted in the tables which follow.

†"Strong" means that the party's legislative candidate at the previous general election (1956 except for the 17 senators elected in 1954) polled at least 55 per cent of the total vote.

‡The large number of retired and indefinite in the occupational category under total membership reflects a lack of specificity in replies to Blue Book questions by the same legislators who failed to reply at all to the author's questionnaire.

TABLE VI-C
LEGISLATIVE AGE DISTRIBUTION (1957)

Party	All Legislators						
	-35	36-45	46-55	56-65	66+	Indef.	Total
Republicans	18	14	15	20	20	3	90
Democrats	7	14	12	6	3	1	43
Total	25	28	27	26	23	4	133
	Urban Legislators						
Republicans	10	3	3	7	3	1	27
Democrats	7	10	9	4	3	1	34
Total	17	13	12	11	6	2	61
	Rural Legislators						
Republicans	8	11	12	13	17	2	63
Democrats	0	4	3	2	0	0	9
Total	8	15	15	15	17	2	72

TABLE VI-D
DURATION OF LOCAL RESIDENCE OF LEGISLATORS (1957)
(Per Cent)

Years in county	Urban legislators	Rural legislators	Total
1-10	2.0	6.6	4.5
11-20	12.0	4.9	8.1
21-30	16.0	14.8	15.3
31-	70.0	73.8	72.1
Total	100.0	100.1	100.0
Years in district			
1-10	14.0	6.6	9.9
11-20	16.0	3.3	9.0
21-30	18.0	14.8	16.2
31-	52.0	75.4	64.9
Total	100.0	100.1	100.0
Number	50	61	111

TABLE VI-E
LEGISLATIVE SERVICE (1957)
(Per Cent)

Term	Urban Assemblymen	Urban Senators	Rural Assemblymen	Rural Senators	All
First	34.0	57.1	24.5	26.3	31.6
Second	25.5	21.4	26.4	26.3	25.6
Third	10.6	14.3	15.1	21.1	14.3
Fourth	8.5	0.0	7.5	15.8	8.3
Fifth	8.5	0.0	9.4	10.5	8.3
Sixth or more	12.8	7.1	17.0	0.0	12.0
Total	99.9	99.9	99.9	100.0	100.1
Number	47	14	53	19	133

TABLE VI-F
PREVIOUS ELECTION OF LEGISLATORS (1957) TO OTHER
PUBLIC OFFICES (Per Cent)

Elected to other office	Urban	Rural	Rep.	Dem.	All
Yes	34.0	65.6	63.2	25.7	51.4
No	66.0	32.8	35.5	74.3	47.8
Indefinite	0.0	1.6	1.3	0.0	0.9
Total	100.0	100.0	100.0	100.0	100.1
Number	50	61	76	35	111

TABLE VI-G
ELECTION DEFEATS OF LEGISLATORS (1957) IN PREVIOUS
ATTEMPTS FOR LEGISLATIVE OR OTHER OFFICE
(Per Cent)

Defeated for other office	Urban	Rural	Rep.	Dem.	All
Yes	46.0	47.5	46.1	48.6	46.8
No	54.0	49.2	51.3	51.4	51.4
Indefinite	0.0	3.3	2.6	0.0	1.8
Total	100.0	100.0	100.0	100.0	100.0
Number	50	61	76	35	111

TABLE VI-H
EDUCATION OF LEGISLATORS (1957)
(Per Cent)

Education completed	Urban	Rural	Rep.	Dem.	All
Less than high school	11.5	22.2	17.8	16.3	17.3
High school	21.3	18.1	18.9	20.9	19.5
Some college	14.8	13.9	14.4	14.0	14.3
College degree	11.5	19.4	16.7	14.0	15.8
Advanced degree	39.3	26.4	32.2	32.6	32.3
Indefinite	1.6	0.0	0.0	2.3	0.8
Total	100.0	100.0	100.0	100.1	100.0
Number	61	72	90	43	133

TABLE VI-I
OCCUPATIONS OF LEGISLATORS (L.) AND OF THE FATHERS (F.) OF LEGISLATORS (1957)
(Per Cent)

Occupations	Reps.		Dems.		Urban		Rural		All	
	L.	F.	L.	F.	L.	F.	L.	F.	L.	F.
Lawyers	31.9	9.7	39.4	6.1	41.7	8.3	28.1	8.8	34.3	8.6
Other profs.	5.5	5.5	3.0	18.2	4.2	12.5	5.3	7.0	4.8	9.5
Business-managerial	18.1	8.3	21.2	21.2	18.8	20.8	19.3	5.3	19.0	12.4
Sales-clerical	6.9	8.3	15.2	0.0	14.6	10.4	5.3	1.8	9.5	5.7
Manual workers	1.4	22.2	18.2	36.4	14.6	31.3	0.0	22.8	6.7	26.7
Farmers	31.9	44.4	0.0	18.2	2.1	14.6	38.6	54.4	21.9	36.2
Local gov't. officials	0.0	1.4	3.0	0.0	2.1	2.1	0.0	0.0	1.0	1.0
Indefinite	4.2	0.0	0.0	0.0	2.1	0.0	3.5	0.0	2.9	0.0
Total	99.9	99.8	100.0	100.1	100.2	100.0	100.1	100.1	100.1	100.1
Number*	72	72	33	33	48	48	57	57	105	105

*The total of respondents is 105 instead of 111, as in the case of other questionnaire items, because of the omission of six legislators who were imprecise about their fathers' occupations. In most of these instances, fathers were listed as having died very early in life.

TABLE VI-J
LEGISLATORS SUBSEQUENTLY HOLDING HIGHER PARTISAN
OFFICES, 1925-1955

Office	Total holding office	Former legs. holding office	Mean av. years of leg. service	Mean av. age of leg. entry
U.S. Senator	7	2	5	33.0
Governor	10	3	4.7	42.3
Other state constit. officer	26	8	8.6	39.0
U.S. Representative	49	16	4.7	35.0

TABLE VI-K
FORMER LEGISLATORS HOLDING ELECTED
JUDGESHIPS (1955)

Judgeship	Total no. of judges	Former legs.
State supreme court	7	1
Circuit court	22	2
County court	72	2
Special court	40	1

TABLE VI-L
LOSING CANDIDACIES OF LEGISLATORS AND FORMER
LEGISLATORS FOR HIGHER PARTISAN
OFFICES, 1924—1954*

Office	No. of elections	Leg. losers in primary	Leg. losers in gen. el.
U.S. Senator	10	5	3
Governor	16	10	8
Other state constit. officer	64	26	14
U.S. Representative	164	57	50
Total	254	98	75

*Since this is a count of candidacies, legislators and former legislators who lost more than once are counted more than once. Also it should be explained that the number of elections is calculated by counting a primary and a general election for the same office in a given year as one election (not two).

TABLE VI-M
FORMER LEGISLATORS REGISTERED AS LOBBYISTS
COMPARED TO TOTAL NUMBER
OF LOBBYISTS, 1949–1955

Leg. session	Total no. of lobbyists	No. of former legislators reg. as lobbyists	Per cent
1949	222	18	8.1
1951	221	20	9.0
1953	252	24	9.5
1955	292	22	7.5

TABLE VI-N
EX-LEGISLATORS, 1919-1953, REGISTERED AS
LOBBYISTS, 1921-1955

	Number	Number Registered	Percentage
Lawyers	152	55	36.2
Nonlawyers	711	96	13.5
	863	151	17.5

TABLE VII-A
CENSUS-DEFINED URBAN AND RURAL CLASSIFICATION
OF LEGISLATIVE DISTRICTS, ACCORDING
TO PARTY (1957)*

Population status of districts	Assembly			Senate		
	Rep.	Dem.	Total	Rep.	Dem.	Total
Over 1/2 rural	41	7	48	14	1	15
1/3 to 1/2 rural	5	0	5	4	2	6
Less than 1/3 rural	21	26	47	5	7	12
Total	67	33	100	23	10	33

*In this table only, of all those in Chapters Six and Seven, "urban" and "rural" are used in the strict U.S. Census terminology—that is, "urban" means those living in places of 2,500 or more plus those in urbanized places. Otherwise, in the tables which follow, "urban" and "rural" are as defined in the first note of Table VI-A, although Table VII-B presents a refinement based on that definition.

TABLE VII-B
MODIFIED URBAN AND RURAL CLASSIFICATION OF LEGISLATIVE DISTRICTS, ACCORDING TO PARTY (1957)

Population status of districts	Assembly			Senate		
	Rep.	Dem.	Total	Rep.	Dem.	Total
Over 1/2 in urbanized areas and other cities over 50,000	9	25	34	4	8	12
Over 1/2 in cities of 10,000 to 50,000	12	1	13	2	-	2
Over 1/2 in places under 10,000 (including farms)	46	7	53	17	2	19
Total	67	33	100	23	10	33

TABLE VII-C
COMPETITION IN ASSEMBLY DISTRICTS, 1956

Vote polled by winning party candidates for governor and assemblyman, 1956	Party holding district		Total
	Rep.	Dem.	
Above 60 per cent	19	12	31
55–60 per cent	21	12	33
52–55 per cent	11	3	14
Below 52 per cent (for one or both offices)	16	6	22
Total	67	33	100

197

TABLE VII-D
LEGISLATORS NOT RE-ELECTED, 1946-1956

Year	Defeated in primary	Defeated in gen. el.	Not seeking re-election	Total
Assembly				
1946	20	3	16	39
1948	10	9	20	39
1950	17	6	11	34
1952	8	4	11	23
1954	7	6	26	39
1956	8	4	20	32
Total	70	32	104	206
Senate				
1946	2	1	3	6
1948	3	2	6	11
1950	1	1	2	4
1952	0	0	5	5
1954	3	0	8	11
1956	0	0	8	8
Total	9	4	32	45
Assembly and Senate				
Grand total	79	36	136	251
Per cent	31.5	14.3	54.2	100.0

TABLE VII-E
ASSEMBLY CONTESTS IN PRIMARY AND GENERAL ELECTIONS, 1946-1956

Election	Rep. primary		Dem. primary		General el.	
	No.	%	No.	%	No.	%
Contested	321	53.5	140	23.3	513	85.5
Uncontested*	267	44.5	375	62.5	87	14.5
No candidate	12	2.0	85	14.2	0	0.0
Total	600	100.0	600	100.0	600	100.0

*Elections are counted as uncontested when a losing candidate received fewer than 75 votes.

TABLE VII-F
ASSEMBLY CANDIDATES ELECTED WITHOUT OPPOSITION IN BOTH PRIMARY AND GENERAL ELECTIONS, 1946-1956

Year	Party		Incumbency		Total
	Rep.	Dem.	Inc.	Not inc.	
1946	7	1	7	1	8
1948	7	1	8	0	8
1950	2	1	3	0	3
1952	6	1	7	0	7
1954	3	3	5	1	6
1956	6	2	8	0	8
Total	31	9	38	2	40

TABLE VII-G
ASSEMBLY PRIMARY CONTESTS RELATIVE TO
INCUMBENCY, 1946–1956

Primary	Total no. of elections	Per cent contested
Republican		
with Rep. incumbent	381	50.4
without Rep. incumbent	219	58.9
Democratic		
with Dem. incumbent	118	48.3
without Dem. incumbent	582	14.3

TABLE VII-H
PRIMARY CONTESTS IN RELATION TO GENERAL
ELECTION VOTE: PROPORTIONS OF DEMOCRATIC
AND REPUBLICAN ASSEMBLY NOMINATIONS
CONTESTED, 1956, IN RELATION TO 1956 GENERAL
ELECTION VOTE IN ASSEMBLY DISTRICTS

Nominees' general election percentage	Democratic		Republican	
	Number of nomi- nations	Per cent* contested	Number of nomi- nations	Per cent* contested
Under 40	28	7.1	18	22.2
40–44	12	33.3	3	33.3
45–49	17	41.2	7	14.3
50–54	7	42.9	17	58.8
55–59	2	100.0	14	71.4
60 and over	24	58.3	35	42.9

*The numbers in some of the cells are too small for the percentages to be meaningful.

TABLE VII-I
ASSEMBLY PRIMARY CONTESTS IN RELATION TO
PARTY COMPETITION, 1954 AND 1956

Districts*	No.	Per cent contested, 1954	Per cent contested, 1956
Democratic Primary			
Strong Rep.	40	10.0	12.5
Marginal	36	36.1	38.9
Strong Dem.	24	41.7	54.2
Total	100	27.0	32.0
Republican Primary			
Strong Dem.	24	25.0	12.5
Marginal	36	58.3	38.9
Strong Rep.	40	47.5	60.0
Total	100	46.0	41.0

*"Strong" is here defined to mean 55 per cent or more of
the votes polled by a given party's candidates for governor
and for the Assembly in 1956.

TABLE VII-J
MINORITY WINNERS IN ASSEMBLY ELECTIONS,
1946–1956

Year	Minority winner in primary*	Also won general election	Total Assembly seats
1946	34	28	100
1948	31	22	100
1950	24	18	100
1952	20	12	100
1954	28	25	100
1956	15	13	100
Total	152	118	600
Per cent	---	19.7	100.0

*"Minority winner" is defined as any winning primary candidate who received fewer than 50 per cent of the votes cast.

TABLE VII-K
MARGINS OF WINNING CANDIDATES IN CONTESTED
ASSEMBLY PRIMARIES, 1954 AND 1956

Primary	Total contests	Contests won by less than 2 to 1 margin*
Democratic		
1954	27	22
1956	32	24
Republican		
1954	46	36
1956	41	33

*The margin of 2 to 1 refers to the margin of the winning candidate over his nearest opponent if there was more than one opponent.

TABLE VII-L
UNCONTESTED LEGISLATIVE SEATS IN GENERAL
ELECTIONS, 1900–1956*

Year	Senate	Assembly	
1900	0	1	
1902	1	3	
1904	0	2	
			Primary law
1906	3	2	
1908	1	3	
1910	0	2	
1912	0	2	
1914	1	1	
1916	2	6	
1918	5	22	
1920	6	21	
1922	6	35	
1924	6	26	
1926	8	39	
1928	2	17	
1930	4	30	
1932	0	1	
1934	0	0	
1936	0	1	
1938	0	0	
1940	0	0	
1942	2	16	
1944	4	26	
1946	6	26	
1948	3	19	
1950	0	6	
1952	2	17	
1954	3	7	
1956	2	12	

*There were always 100 Assembly seats to be filled, and
in the Senate 16 seats in presidential years and 17 in other
years. Seats are counted as uncontested in general elections
if there was no listed party opponent and no Independent
candidate polling more than 100 votes. As late as the 1920's
there were large numbers of minority party candidates,
including many Socialists who were elected, and in the
period 1934–1944 there were third-party Progressives.

TABLE VII-M
MEMBERSHIP OF LEGISLATORS(1957) IN THEIR
PRESENT POLITICAL PARTY
(Per Cent)

Years of membership	Rep.	Dem.	All
0−5	10.5	28.6	16.2
6−10	11.8	34.3	18.9
11−15	10.5	11.4	10.8
16−20	11.8	5.7	9.9
21−25	6.6	2.9	5.4
26−30	11.8	5.7	9.9
31−35	11.8	0.0	8.1
36−40	10.5	0.0	7.2
41−	10.5	5.7	9.0
Indefinite	3.9	5.7	4.5
Total	99.7	100.0	99.9
Number	76	35	111

TABLE VII-N
ACTIVITY IN PARTY ORGANIZATIONS BY
LEGISLATORS (1957)
(Per Cent)

Activity	Rep.	Dem.	Urban	Rural	All
Party office					
Yes	42.1	62.9	62.0	37.7	48.6
No	55.3	37.1	38.0	59.0	49.5
Indefinite	2.6	0.0	0.0	3.3	1.8
Total	100.0	100.0	100.0	100.0	99.9
Other activity					
Yes	76.3	82.9	78.0	78.7	78.4
No	19.7	17.1	18.0	19.7	18.9
Indefinite	3.9	0.0	4.0	1.6	2.7
Total	99.9	100.0	100.0	100.0	100.0
Number	76	35	50	61	111

TABLE VII-O
VIEW BY LEGISLATORS (1957) OF ROLE OF LOCAL
PARTY LEADERS IN RELATION TO ORIGINAL
LEGISLATIVE NOMINATIONS
(Per Cent)

Party leaders:	Strong Rep.*	Strong Dem.*	Compet- itive	All
Persuaded me to run	10.3	17.2	16.7	13.5
Encouraged me to run	22.4	41.4	20.8	27.0
Favored another candidate	15.5	3.4	12.5	11.7
Some favored me, some did not	22.4	10.3	8.3	16.2
No action at all	25.9	27.6	33.3	27.9
Indefinite	3.4	0.0	8.3	3.6
Total	99.9	99.9	99.9	99.9
Number	58	29	24	111

*"Strong" refers to districts in which the successful
legislative candidate won at least 55 per cent of his last
general election vote.

TABLE VII-P
VIEW BY LEGISLATORS (1957) OF THE CAUSE OF THEIR
ORIGINAL INTEREST IN RUNNING FOR
LEGISLATIVE OFFICE
(Per Cent)

Cause	Strong Rep.*	Strong Dem.*	Compet- itive	All
Own idea	46.6	44.8	66.7	50.5
Suggested by party leaders	15.5	34.5	16.7	20.7
Suggested by friends	31.0	13.8	8.3	21.6
Other or indefinite	6.9	6.9	8.3	7.2
Total	100.0	100.0	100.0	100.0
Number	58	29	24	111

*"Strong" refers to districts in which the successful
legislative candidate won at least 55 per cent of his last
general election vote.

TABLE VII-Q
VIEW BY LEGISLATORS (1957) OF LOCAL PARTY ROLE IN THEIR GENERAL ELECTION CAMPAIGNS
(Per Cent)

Party Role	Rep.	Dem.	Urban	Rural	Strong Rep.*	Strong Dem.*	Competitive	All
No part	17.1	17.1	16.0	18.0	15.5	20.7	16.7	17.1
Some help, but not of great importance	47.4	40.0	42.0	47.5	46.6	37.9	54.2	45.9
Considerable help	32.9	40.0	40.0	31.1	34.5	41.4	25.0	34.2
Indefinite	2.6	2.9	2.0	3.3	3.4	0.0	4.2	2.7
Total	100.0	100.0	100.0	99.9	100.0	100.0	100.1	99.9
Number	76	35	50	61	58	29	24	111

*"Strong" refers to districts in which the successful legislative candidate won at least 55 per cent of the vote at his last general election.

TABLE VII-R
VIEW BY LEGISLATORS (1957) OF CAMPAIGN HELP
BY VARIOUS GROUPS
(Per Cent)*

Helped by:	Rep.	Dem.	All
Party organization	21.1	40.0	27.0
County board	22.4	5.7	17.1
Farm organization	11.8	14.3	12.6
Newspaper	0.0	8.6	2.7
Church or church organization	2.6	2.9	2.7
Veterans' organization	1.3	2.9	1.8
Unions	2.6	37.1	13.5
Conservation club	1.3	0.0	0.9
Chamber of Commerce	7.9	0.0	5.4
Other business group	1.3	2.8	1.8
Friends	15.8	0.0	10.8
None	23.7	2.9	18.9
Indefinite	14.5	8.6	12.6
Number	76	35	111

*Since legislators checked more than one item, the percentages add up to more than 100 per cent in each column.

TABLE VII-S
LEGISLATORS' REPORTS (1957) ON THEIR METHODS
OF CAMPAIGNING WHEN FIRST ELECTED
(Per Cent)*

Method	Urban	Rural	All
Newspaper ads.	54.0	77.0	66.7
Speeches	54.0	41.0	46.8
Radio talks & interviews	10.0	16.4	13.5
Radio spot announcements	14.0	21.3	18.0
TV talks & interviews	6.0	4.9	5.4
TV spot announcements	4.0	3.3	3.6
Door-to-door	62.0	50.8	55.9
Flyers, pamphlets, matches	74.0	50.8	61.3
Party organization help	36.0	19.7	27.0
Help from family	56.0	21.3	36.9
Help from friends	74.0	50.8	61.3
No real campaign	2.0	6.6	4.5
Number	50	61	111

*Because candidates indicated more than one method, the percentages in each column do not total 100 per cent.

Party officer questionnaire

County_____   Party position_____

How many years have you been a member of your political party? _____

How many years have you been an active party worker (fund-raising,
   leadership, circulating nomination papers, etc.)? _____

In 1956 or 1957 has there been a contest for any office in your
   local party organization? _____

Have you ever been a delegate or alternate to a state party convention?
   _____Yes   _____No

Have you ever been a delegate or alternate to a national party convention?
   _____Yes   _____No

Have you ever been elected to public office? _____Yes   _____No
   If so, what office? _____

Have you ever been a losing candidate for elective public office? _____Yes   _____No
   If so, what office? _____

Do you intend to run for elective public office? _____Yes   _____No

Have you any desire ever to run for elective public office? _____Yes   _____No

About how many members were there in your county organization in the election
   year 1956? _____

Which election are you usually most concerned that your party's candidate should win?

   _____President
   _____Governor
   _____U. S. Senator
   _____U. S. Congressman
   _____State Legislator
   _____County courthouse office

What political issues are usually of greatest interest to you?

   _____National issues
   _____State issues
   _____County issues

In your county, which of the following best describes what party leaders like yourself
   usually do with respect to the selection of party candidates for the Wisconsin
   state assembly or state senate?

   _____ Actively seek well-qualified candidates.
   _____ Persuade well-qualified individuals to run.
   _____ Encourage well-qualified individuals to run.
   _____ Try to persuade individuals not to enter the primary against
      a well-qualified candidate already in the race.
   _____ No part at all; individual candidates just come forward on
      their own to run in the primary.

How much opportunity do you have to discuss state legislative work with either your
   state senator or your state assemblyman?

   _____none   _____some
   _____a little   _____a great deal

What is your regular occupation? _____

Questionnaire submitted to legislators

District_____   Party_____

How many years have you lived in your county? _____years

How many years have you lived in your legislative district? _____years

Besides your present office, what other public offices have you been
elected to? _____

_____

What public offices have you run for and not been elected to (even if at another
time you were elected)?_____

_____

How many years have you been a member of your political party? _____years

Have you ever held office in your party organization? _____Yes _____No

Have you been active in your party in any other way? _____Yes _____No

In your own general election campaigns for your legislative position, what part
is usually played by your local party organization? (please check one)
_____ no part (except use of party label) _____ considerable help
_____ some help but not of great importance in my campaign

When you were first elected to your present legislative position, what did your
local party leaders do concerning your nomination in the primary?
(please check one)
_____ persuaded me to run _____ generally favored another candidate
_____ encouraged me to run _____ some favored me, some did not
_____ no action at all

When you were first elected to your present legislative position, how had you
happened to be interested in running? (please check one)
_____ pretty much my own idea _____ suggested by friends
_____ suggested by party leaders _____ other? _____

When you were first elected to your present legislative position, which of the
following methods of campaigning did you use fairly extensively?
(please check as many as are appropriate)
_____ newspaper advertisements _____ door-to-door
_____ speeches at meetings _____ flyers, pamphlets, matches
_____ radio talks & interviews _____ party organizational help
_____ radio spot announcements _____ help from family
_____ television talks & interviews _____ help from friends
_____ television spot announcements _____ no real campaign work

In your own campaigns, what group (such as party organization, farm organization,
union, chamber of commerce, town chairmen, etc.) has usually been of
greatest help--if any group has? _____

_____

What was your father's principal occupation? _____

Was your father in politics (either as a public office-holder, a candidate, or a
party officer)? _____Yes _____No

209

Real estate men: as legislators, 110–11
Reapportionment, legislative. *See* Apportionment, legislative
Recruitment. *See* Candidates
Registration, 24
Religion, 19
Rennebohm, Oscar, 167
Representation, legislative, 121, 122–28, 144. *See also* Apportionment, legislative; Elections, legislative
Republican party: statewide postwar position of, 8–9, 46–56, 147–51; and pre-primary endorsement, 25–26, 55–56, 92–96, 156; and two-party system, 34–35; historical status of, 35–37, 39–40, 164; statewide primary of, 37–40, 50, 55–56, 147, 183; issue orientation of, 44, 82–86, 155; organization of, 51, 77, 80–82; urban vote of, 60–61, 61–66, 66–69, 72–76; metropolitan vote of, 60–61, 61–66, 72–76; small city and village vote of, 60–61, 66–69, 72–76; farm vote of, 60–61, 70–76; and special senatorial election, 72–75; finances of, 78–79; occupations of officers of, 79, 88–89, 96; political generations in, 86–88, 96; local party office contests in, 90; candidacy of leaders of, 90–91; candidate selection by, 92–96; characteristics of legislators of, 106, 108–9, 110, 112; legislative representation of, 124, 125–28, 129, 144, 150; legislative primaries of, 131, 133–35; relation to Republican legislators, 139–42; legislative candidacies of, 152–53; in one-party Republican county, 170–71; age of officers of, 171
Republican Voluntary Committee. *See* Republican party
Residence: of legislators, 99, 106–7, 120, 190
Robinson, W. S., 166

Roosevelt, Franklin D., 41, 43, 88
Roper, Elmo, 167
Rosenstein, Joseph, 168
Rousseau, Jean Jacques, 31
Ruralism: and urbanism, 8; degree of, 13–16; and daylight-saving time, 15–16; and voting, 53, 56, 66–72, 73–76; defined, 59; and party organizations, 81, 89, 90, 91; and legislative districts, 99–100, 104; and characteristics of legislators, 99, 102, 105–11, 120; legislative representation of, 121, 125–26, 144, 196, 197; and Republican representation, 125–28; and primary competition, 133. *See also* Farm population

St. Lawrence seaway, 22
Scandinavians, 18, 19
Schafer, Joseph, 164
Schattschneider, E. E., 177
Schlesinger, Joseph A., 163, 175
Schmitt, Len, 55–56
Selection of candidates. *See* Candidates; Nomination; Primary election
Seligman, Lester, 175
Senate, state: term of office, 23; confirmation of appointees, 26; size of, 26–27, 98; length of service in, 104; districts for, 118; party representation in, 126–28, 150; campaign expenditures for, 143. *See also* Elections, legislative; Legislators
Separation of powers, 123–24, 150
Sheriff: election of, 47–48
Shields, Currin, 169
Shils, Edward A., 111
Smith, George A., 94, 172
Socialist party, 36, 37, 176
Socioeconomic characteristics: and method, 6; of state, 11–22; and size of place, 63–72; of party officers, 79, 81–82, 88–89, 96; of legislators, 99, 105–15, 120, 188; of Milwaukee legislative candidates, 138
Sorauf, Frank J., 170

ground of state legislators, and the method of nominating and electing them. The conclusion explains the significance of the new two-party system in terms of the state's past experience and discusses the question whether this system, as it now operates in Wisconsin, meets the criterion of democratic competition. It also shows how the Wisconsin system compares with a model "responsible" party system.

Mr. Epstein discusses several subjects of current interest: the advantages and disadvantages of the open primary, why it became established in Wisconsin, and how it affects present voting; the way in which the party organizations function in the selection of candidates; and the differences between urban and rural political practices.

The author, a political scientist whose chief interest is in general political ideas, has written a book which will be helpful to Wisconsin journalists and politicians, as well as to politically conscious laymen. This wider public will find it especially rewarding to consider the analysis of the 1956 election and the special election of 1957. Students of politics in other states will be interested in the method Mr. Epstein uses in working out his analysis and in his frequent references to the ways in which the Wisconsin system compares with others. For both lay readers and specialists the value of the work is enhanced by the fact that it is based on more statistical data, largely from election returns, and on more interviews and questionnaires than are most other books which deal with the politics of a single state.

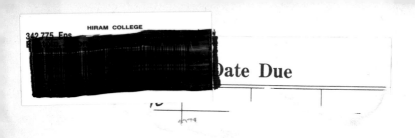

Date Due